BERKLEE PRESS

JOE STUMP'S

METAL GUITAR CHOP SHOP

BUILDING SHRED & METAL TECHNIQUE

To access audio visit:
www.halleonard.com/mylibrary

Enter Code
7860-7687-0523-5171

Berklee Press

Editor in Chief: Jonathan Feist
Vice President of Online Learning and Continuing Education: Debbie Cavalier
Assistant Vice President of Operations for Berklee Media: Robert F. Green
Assistant Vice President of Marketing and Recruitment for Berklee Media: Mike King
Dean of Continuing Education: Carin Nuernberg
Editorial Assistants: Matthew Dunkle, Reilly Garrett, Zoë Lustri
Cover Design: Kathy Kikkert
Cover Photo: Eddie Carlino

ISBN 978-0-87639-146-4

1140 Boylston Street
Boston, MA 02215-3693 USA
(617) 747-2146

Visit Berklee Press Online at
www.berkleepress.com

Study with

■ **BERKLEE ONLINE**

online.berklee.edu

DISTRIBUTED BY

HAL•LEONARD®
CORPORATION
7777 W. BLUEMOUND RD. P.O. BOX 13819
MILWAUKEE, WISCONSIN 53213

Visit Hal Leonard Online at
www.halleonard.com

Berklee Press, a publishing activity of Berklee College of Music, is a not-for-profit educational publisher.
Available proceeds from the sales of our products are contributed to the scholarship funds of the college.

CONTENTS

AUDIO

Recording Note: On the audio, my guitar is tuned one half step down to concert E-flat. I've always used this tuning on all of my solo releases. Being a half step down gives the guitar a slightly different feel, string tension-wise. It also sounds a little heavier in the slightly lower tuning.

Gearwise, on these tracks, I used my ESP custom shop Strats with scalloped fingerboards and Dimarzio pickups, played thru Marshall amplification.

Go to www.halleonard.com/mylibrary and enter the code found on the first page of this book to access the accompanying audio examples. This will grant you instant access to every example. The examples that include audio are marked with an audio icon throughout the book.

TITLE

TITLE

TITLE

ACKNOWLEDGMENTS

I'd just like to thank my great sources of continual inspiration: Ritchie Blackmore, Yngwie Malmsteen, Gary Moore, Uli Jon Roth, Michael Schenker, Jimi Hendrix, J.S. Bach, Antonio Vivaldi, Ludwig van Beethoven, Niccolò Paganini, Pyotr Ilyich Tchaikovsky, and C.P.E. Bach. Your tremendous impact and influence on my playing helped shape much of the material contained in this book.

Also, of course, a huge thanks to all my fans worldwide. Your continued support is greatly appreciated.

Joe Stump on the Web:

JoeStump.com

facebook.com/JoeShredlordStump

facebook.com/pages/Joe-Stumps-Fan-Page/191898544232444

CHAPTER 1

Scale Fingerings and Technique-Building Studies

In this chapter, I'll be showing multiple ways to finger the natural minor scale, also known as the Aeolian mode—one of the most common scales used in hard rock and metal. In addition to the scale fingerings themselves, I'll be showing several easy technique-building studies that will not only help with speed and technical command, but also be helpful in committing the scale fingerings to memory.

MINOR SCALE FINGERINGS

Figures 1.1 and 1.2 are very standard ways to finger the minor scale involving playing the root of the scale on the six string with your first finger. These first two fingerings have a combination of three notes on some strings and two notes on others. There are many different reasons why it's beneficial to know multiple ways to finger a set of tones. It helps you to know the neck and understand the instrument better. Also, different types of runs and single-note melodic ideas are conducive to certain left-hand shapes, so the more fingerings you know, the more options are available to you.

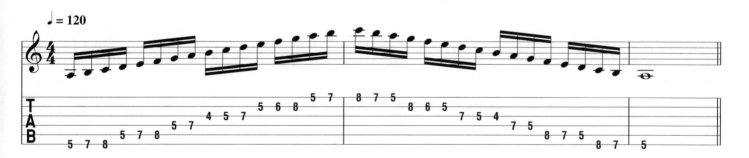

FIG. 1.1. Minor Scale Fingering 1

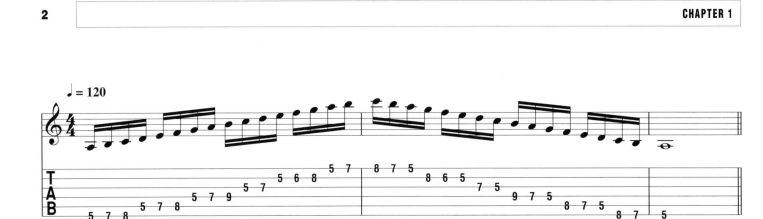

FIG. 1.2. Minor Scale Fingering 2

Speed Scales: Three Notes Per String

One very common way for rock and metal players to finger scales is with three notes on each string. The concept is quite easy: play only the notes in the scale, and play three notes on each string. These are also known as speed scales. With the symmetrical three-note-per-string shape, it's quite easy to play across the strings, both ascending and descending, very fast. You can apply this concept to any scale or mode. Since I'm a metal player, I gravitate towards the darker sounding minor scales: natural minor/Aeolian, harmonic minor, Phrygian Dominant, Hungarian minor, double harmonic minor, etc.

Root on the 6th String Using the First Finger

Figure 1.3 is the A minor speed-scale fingering with the root of the scale on the 6th string with the first finger. While the actual scale starts and ends on A, first in one octave (4th string 7th fret) then to a second octave (2nd string 10th fret), it's very common to practice the entire six-string shape. As far as practicing the scale goes, it's helpful to play up and down the scale in different rhythms using a metronome (eighth notes/two notes per beat, triplets/three notes per beat, sixteenth notes/ four notes per beat, sextuplets/six notes per beat). With three notes on each string, it's quite easy to play the scale in triplets or sextuplets (sixteenth-note triplets).

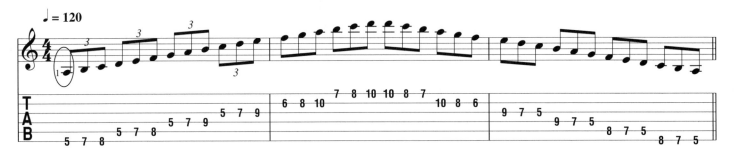

FIG. 1.3. Root on the 6th String Using the First Finger

Root on 6th String Using the Second Finger

In figure 1.4, I'm still playing the natural minor scale with the root on the 6th string, but this time, the root is played with my second finger. In order to execute the entire six-string shape, start on G (6th string 3rd fret). While this, of course, could imply another scale/mode (G Mixolydian), it is a very valid shape for A minor as well. Also, the scale root (note that the scale's named for) doesn't always have to be on the 6th string with your first finger. If that were the case, we'd be very limited navigating throughout the neck.

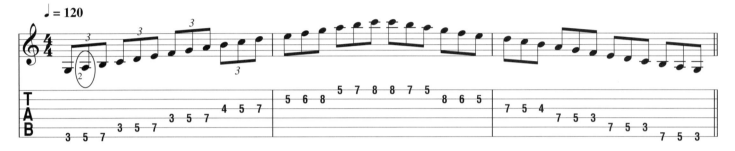

FIG. 1.4. Root on 6th String Using the Second Finger

Root on the 5th String Using the First Finger

In figure 1.5, the root of the scale is now on the 5th string with the first finger. When playing the entire six-string shape, you'd be starting on E (6th string 12th fret), also implying another mode (E Phrygian). But once again, this is a very cool/valid fingering for A natural minor. This fingering also enables you to play the scale in an entirely different area of the guitar.

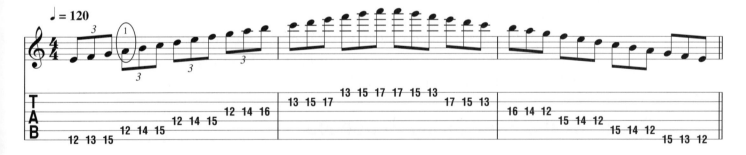

FIG. 1.5. Root on the 5th String Using the First Finger

Root on the 5th String Using the Second Finger

In figure 1.6, the root is on the 5th string once again, this time played with the second finger. The entire shape starts on D (6th string 10th fret) and does imply several other modes (D Dorian/E Phrygian root with second finger). But once again, in this section, we're focusing on thinking of all these shapes in relation to the A natural minor scale.

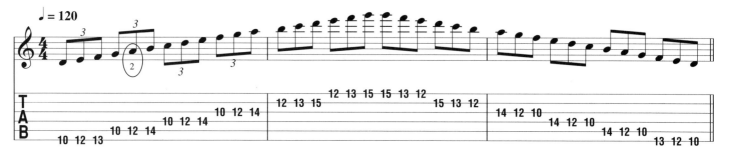

FIG. 1.6. Root on the 5th String Using the Second Finger

TECHNIQUE-BUILDING STUDIES

Many players, while developing, have an extremely hard time committing scale fingerings to memory. These upcoming technical studies are designed to help you memorize fingering shapes while also building speed and technical command, in the process.

The idea is to practice something that helps your technique and chops, but not have it so complex that it distracts from internalizing the speed-scale fingerings. If you are already familiar with these shapes, use these drills to torque up fingerings that you're already comfortable with, or use them to internalize more difficult left-hand scale shapes.

How fast should you practice them, you ask? After committing the studies to memory, it's best to play them consistently at challenging speeds but ones you're in complete command and control of.

Speed Scale: Four-String Sequence

Figure 1.7 features the A minor speed scale played in a four-string sequence. The pattern is easy; just ascend in two groups of four strings (6th string to 3rd string, then 4th string to 1st string). Then descending, it's just the same pattern in reverse (top string to 4th string, then 3rd string to 6th).

The pattern is written in sixteenth-note triplets (six notes per beat), but you can also practice this pattern in triplets (three notes per beat).

Picking-wise, the standard way to execute this would be using alternate picking starting on a down stroke, then continuing with alternate strokes. But you can also *economy-pick* this pattern, starting on a down stroke and playing down/up/down across all six strings, approaching each string with a down stroke. Then descending, it would be the same pattern in reverse; starting on the top string, it would be up/down/up. Or, what I do is economy-pick the ascending portion of the run, and then alternate-pick the descending portion—a combination of the two picking styles.

You can also play this example legato using hammer-ons and pull-offs. Ascending, pick the first note, then hammer on the next two on each string. Descending, pick once and pull off the next two notes. This is an easy way to help strengthen your fretting hand.

On all these technique-building examples, only one fingering type is given, but you can play all of these examples utilizing any type of three-note-per-string mode, in any key, any fingering. You can also combine speed-scale shapes, playing up one fingering then down the following one or try looping them several at a time.

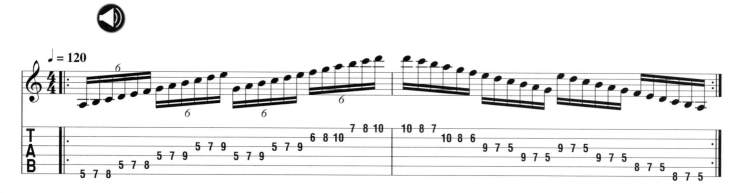

FIG. 1.7. Four-String Sequence

Four-String Sequence with Alternate-Picked Double Up

Figure 1.8 contains the same four-string pattern played in figure 1.7, except this time, I'm doubling up each set of tones on each string, playing them twice using alternate picking. This one's very useful for both pick-hand development and internalizing the left-hand shape.

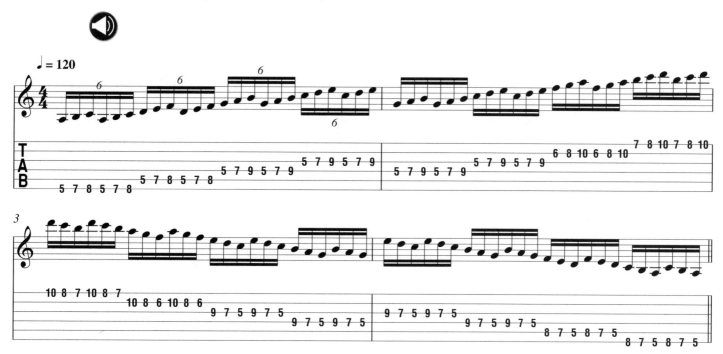

FIG. 1.8. Four-String Sequence with Alternate-Picked Double Up

Double Up and Scale Run Combination

Figure 1.9 is a combination of both 1.7 and 1.8, where the doubled-up pattern is combined with the four-string run. I double up on the 6th and 5th string and then play the four-string run. The pattern repeats on the top four strings, doubling up on strings 4 and 3 then playing the ascending run. Descending, it's the same exact pattern reversed. You can see that now, it's starting to sound a bit more like a possible soloing idea as opposed to just a technical exercise.

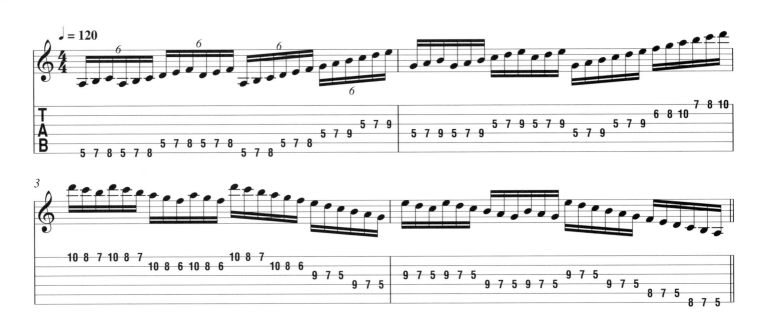

FIG. 1.9. Double Up and Scale Run Combination

Alternate-Picked Scale Fragment with Four-String Climb

Figure 1.10 is very much a soloing type of idea. I take a two-beat, twelve-note alternate picking fragment, and then go back to the 6th string for the four-string run. The same pattern repeats itself on the top four strings. Unlike the other examples, this one is completely different descending. Going down, play a two-beat twelve-note single-string alternate-picking scale fragment, and then the four-string run. The pattern then repeats on strings 3 to 6 descending.

SCALE FRAGMENTS

By *scale fragments*, I mean taking a small section of the scale and playing it in a particular pattern. Many times, these are conducive to being played repeatedly in a circle. Scale fragments can be one beat long, two beats long, four beats long, etc., or cover one to several measures. They can be on a single string or on sets of strings.

Many shredders, myself included, create fast runs that combine various scale fragments. They're a very useful tool in soloing. I'll discuss them in much greater detail in an upcoming chapter, as well as provide examples of combined scale fragments that can be used in a soloing context.

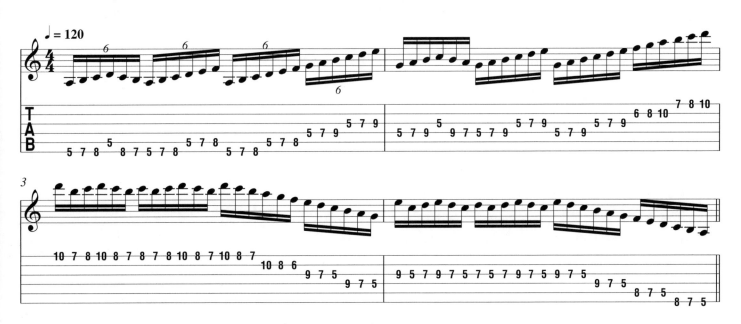

FIG. 1.10. Alternate-Picked Scale Fragment with Four-String Climb

Sixteenth-Note Perpetual Speed-Scale Pattern

Up until now, all of our technique-building examples have been in sixteenth-note triplets (or eighth-note triplets, if you like, depending upon how you're practicing them). These all contain three notes on each string, which is very common.

In figure 1.11, play the scale in straight, even, sixteenth notes (four notes per beat). This is a great picking exercise, crossing over all six strings. Playing it in a circular fashion repeatedly, or navigating it through several left-hand shapes, are very cool ways to practice this one.

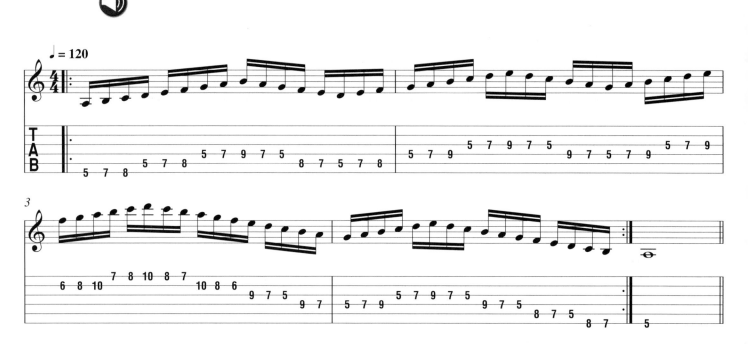

FIG. 1.11. Sixteenth-Note Perpetual Speed-Scale Pattern

CHAPTER 2

Tremolo Picking

Tremolo picking means picking a note multiple times. It is a very easy and natural way for just about any player to alternate-pick at a relatively fast speed. You can practice this technique to build pick-hand speed and endurance, or to memorize scale/arpeggio fingerings, or use it to create solo ideas and riffs. Many players tremolo-pick scale patterns, ascending runs, arpeggios, metal riffs, etc.

TECHNIQUE

If I asked you to play a fast run in sixteenth notes, crossing all six strings, navigating several scalar patterns while alternate picking, that would be quite challenging. But if I said, "Just play straight up and down a scale fingering, playing each scale tone four times each while alternate picking," that would be considerably easier. It is a way that just about any player can alternate with some degree of speed.

Tremolo Picking the A Minor Scale

Figure 2.1 illustrates playing up and down the A natural minor scale, picking each scale tone four times while alternate picking starting on a down stroke. With all of these studies/examples, it's important to use a metronome to ensure playing everything evenly and in time. Plus, a metronome is an excellent device for measuring your progress and technical development.

This pattern is quite easy to alternate-pick, as you approach each new scale tone, as well as each string cross, on a down stroke. For almost all players, it is very natural. It's also a way that even players just starting to develop their technical skill can play sixteenth notes at a relatively high speed.

All of these examples will help build pick-hand strength and alternate-picking consistency. They're also very helpful to players who are just starting to use a metronome. Take note: in the next few examples, I've included several different fingerings for the natural minor scale.

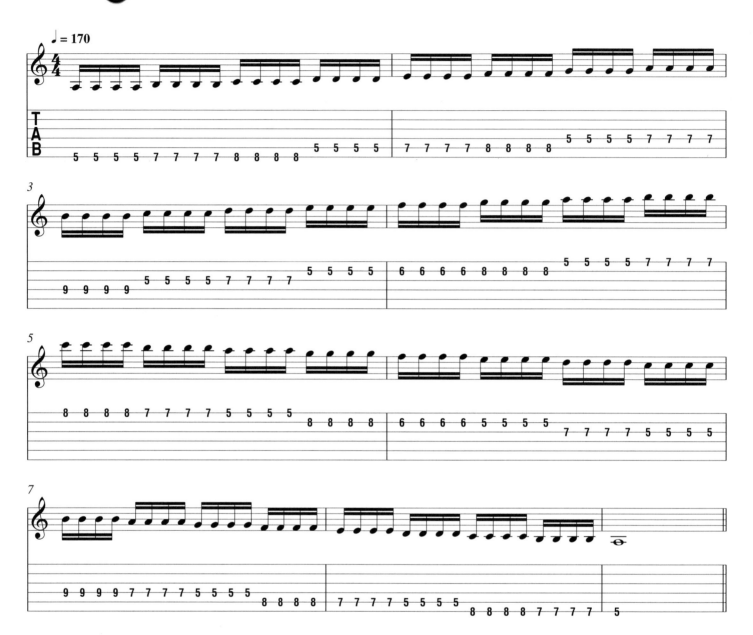

FIG. 2.1. Tremolo Picking: All Strings

Tremolo Picking the A Minor Scale Using Single Strings

Figure 2.2 is a very useful study for tremolo picking up the A natural minor scale/ Aeolian mode on the 1st string, then down the scale on the 2nd string. I've only illustrated the top two strings in this, but you could take this study up and down all six strings in A minor, or do it in varying scales/modes and keys, as well. It's a great way to see the scale up and down each string, all over the neck, as well as help your pick hand. Anytime you can practice something that improves technique, helps you gain knowledge of the instrument, and can be used as soloing/riff vocabulary, it's an excellent thing.

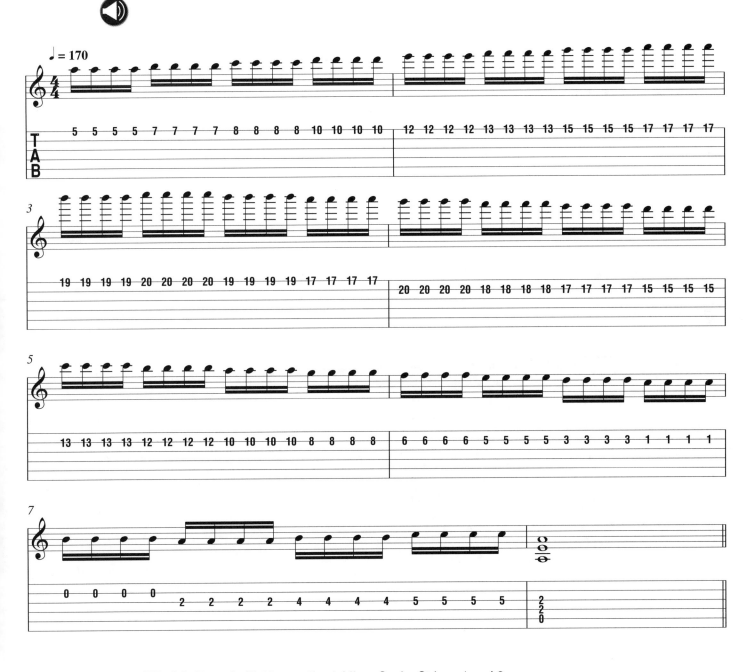

FIG. 2.2. Tremolo Picking on the A Minor Scale: Strings 1 and 2

Tremolo Picking in Triplets

In figure 2.3, the scale is once again tremolo picked, this time hitting each scale tone three times, in triplets. This is a bit trickier, because while alternate-picking this pattern, you're playing down/up/down then up/down/up. So at times, you'll be attacking each new scale tone on an upstroke in addition to also crossing over strings using an upstroke with the pick. A very useful way to sync up both playing and feeling triplets.

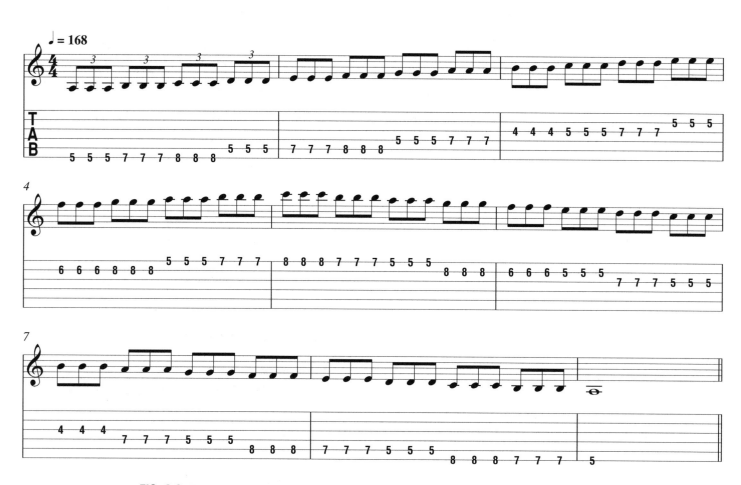

FIG. 2.3. Tremolo Picking with Triplets

Double Picking on the A Minor Scale

Figure 2.4 involves *double picking*—playing each note in the scale two times, but in sixteenth notes, rhythmically. It's a very cool violin type of technique that's great for right- and left-hand synchronization and useful in creating cool riffs and solo ideas. With this even figure, you're once again automatically approaching each new scale tone and string cross on a down stroke, so in many ways, it's like the first example: an easy way to pick alternately without even thinking about it. However, you'll definitely find this pattern considerably more difficult than figure 2.1. With only striking each note twice, it's tougher to sync up at faster tempos.

It's great to practice all these examples with and without palm muting, depending on your personal tastes and also how you'd like them to sound.

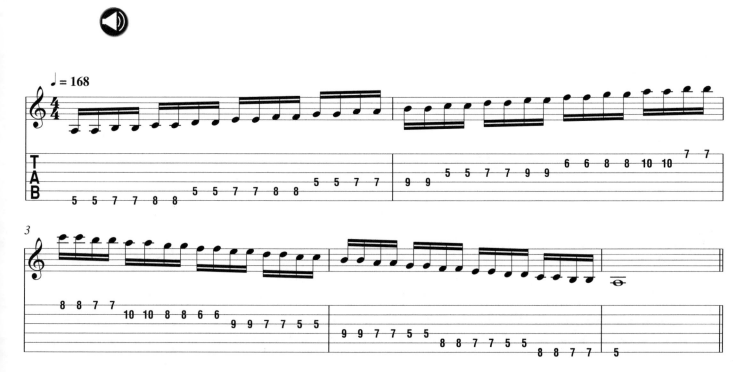

FIG. 2.4. Double Picking

TREMOLO AND DOUBLE PICKING FOR SOLOS

The upcoming examples display tremolo/double picking in a more riff/solo type of context. Hopefully, some of these will help you create your own tremolo-picking riffs, solo ideas, etudes, and drills.

Tremolo-Picked Riff

Figure 2.5 is a speed metal/black metal, extremely fast, tremolo-picked riff that uses one of my favorite scales, Hungarian minor. The Hungarian minor scale is constructed by sharpening both the 4th and 7th degrees of the natural minor scale: A, B, C, D♯, E, F, G♯. Depending upon how it's used, it can be both Eastern and also somewhat evil sounding. The tempo marking on all these upcoming examples is just there to give you an idea of the speeds at which I play these types of exercises. Just concentrate on playing all the examples cleanly, evenly, and in time, and build up the tempo as your technique improves.

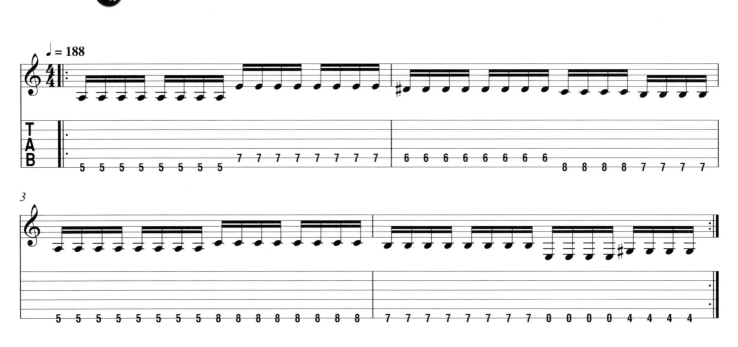

FIG. 2.5. Tremolo-Picked Riff

Tremolo Picking through Arpeggio Shapes

Figure 2.6 involves tremolo picking through arpeggio shapes in triplets. This example is very classical sounding and involves the E harmonic minor scale, a natural minor scale with a raised 7th degree (leading tone): E, F♯, G, A, B, C, D♯. The first arpeggio is E minor, then to a D♯ diminished 7 arpeggio, then an A♯ diminished 7 arpeggio, and lastly, returning to a small harmonic minor run. The arpeggio play combined with the tremolo-triplet picking makes this one a bit more involved, while crossing strings.

FIG. 2.6. Tremolo Picking through Arpeggio Shapes

Double-Picked Solo

Figure 2.7 is a short, double-picked solo type of idea, combining the natural minor and blues scales. This one sounds especially cool with a heavier palm mute. It incorporates double picking down the scale in diatonic thirds (playing a tone in the scale then playing a note a diatonic third, two scale tones away) in measure 4 of the lick. Since there's less string crossing involved and the left-hand shapes are fairly easy, this one might not be as difficult to work up, speed-wise.

FIG. 2.7. Double-Picked Solo in A Minor

Neo-Classical Double Picking

Figure 2.8 is a Baroque, neo-classical double-pick, once again using the E harmonic minor scale. I first climb up the scale in groups of four notes and then descend in thirds, double-picking throughout. I'll have a much more detailed explanation of diatonic scale patterns in chapter 4, along with many cool ways they can be used for melodic sequences, soloing ideas, and chop building.

FIG. 2.8. Neo-Classical Double Picking on the E Harmonic Minor Scale

Single-String Climb

Figure 2.9 is a fast, single-string climb up the A minor scale. The pattern is in sixteenth-note triplets (six notes per beat) and a good example of how fast tremolo picking can be used as an effective soloing tool. While it's a fast run, since you're on one string for most of it, you might surprise yourself as to how easy this one might be for working up the tempo.

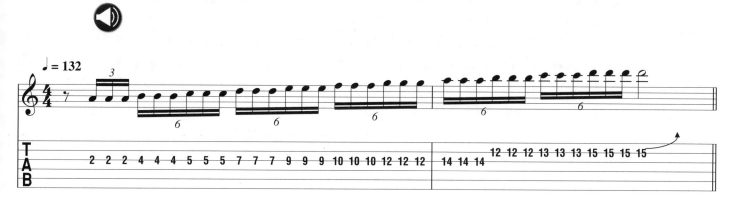

FIG. 2.9. Single-String Climb on the A Minor Scale

CHAPTER 3

"European Metal Double-Picking Etude"

This Euro-metal double-picking etude is a solo (complete with a backing track) comprised of ideas from my tune "The Ultraviolence," off my debut solo record *Guitar Dominance!* (Leviathan Records, 1993/2003). The rhythm guitar part is inspired by classic metal bands like Iron Maiden, Helloween, Hammerfall, and Dio. The solo first incorporates double picking, and then continues combining a variety of metal soloing techniques: pentatonic play, alternate picking, sweep picking, and 2–3 string arpeggio play. It's always more fun and inspiring to practice and learn something that sounds like a section of a tune, as it gives you the real feeling of what these techniques sound like in context.

The rhythm part in figure 3.1 is all in D natural minor, with the exception of the A major chord, which is borrowed from the D harmonic minor scale (very common in metal). It starts with playing a sixteenth-note based metal rhythm, combining power chords with fast, alternate-picked single-note lines connecting the chords. The first chord is D minor; then in bar 2, there's an alternate-picked scale fragment in 5th position, using the root/5 fingering of the D natural minor scale. Bar 3 goes to B-flat major, and then a descending scale pattern, going down in what I call *seconds*—playing a note in the scale then the next higher scale tone.

In the next two bars, it goes to C major, and then a scale pattern inside D minor starting on C climbing up the scale four notes at a time. All the single-note play is, of course, alternate picked. The last two measures contain the climb and the final chord is an A major with the third of the chord (C♯) in the bass. This is a very common chord used in hard rock and metal, showing that there are varying ways to voice triads without the root of the chord in the bass—a very useful inversion to add to your chord and riff arsenal.

A good way to start learning the rhythm part is by first playing just the figure in bar 1, and then going through the entire chord sequence minus the single-note fills. That'll give you a good idea of the feel and vibe of the track. After getting that rocking, you can add in the fills.

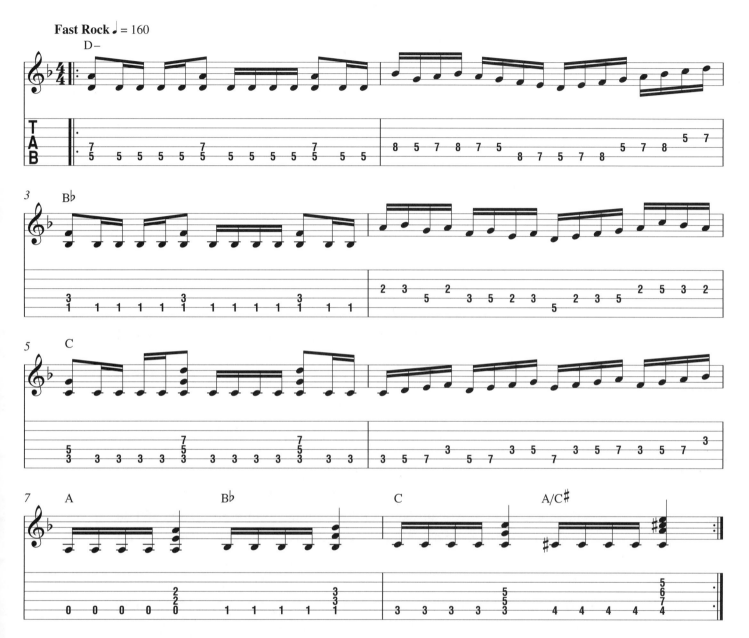

FIG. 3.1. "European Metal Double-Picking Etude," Rhythm Part

Double Picking the Solo Section

The first twenty-four bars of the solo are almost exclusively double picked (except bars 15 and 16, which involve sweep picking). All of this section involves double picking through various small arpeggio shapes that follow suit with the chord sequence. You'll find it very helpful playing straight-sixteenth notes for all twenty-four bars, as it aids in both technical command and endurance. Practicing straight sixteenths also helps you learn some of these small arpeggio shapes you might not be as familiar with. In the first eight bars, all of these arpeggio shapes are on strings 4 and 3. The only additional notes added other than those of the chord are taken from the D natural minor and harmonic minor scales. In bars 9 through 14, I continue the same arpeggio-picking motif using the next higher inversions of all the arpeggios. Then in bars 15 and 16, on the climb, there's some sweep picking involved. These are fairly simple four-string arpeggio sweeps. (Note that on the A/C♯, I'm using a C♯ diminished arpeggio.) Start on the 4th string with a down stroke, then play all downs until you reach your second note on the top string. Then change your pick stroke to an up, pull-off, and then descend with all upstrokes. You might need to isolate this section and practice it slowly, before playing it in context with the rest of the solo, depending on how proficient your sweep picking is. One good way of practicing this is just playing all the arpeggios of the climb individually, multiple times. Then, try them in succession.

Bars 17 to 24 have some lower one-octave arpeggio shapes on strings 5, 4, and 3. The climb in bars 23 and 24 involves a very cool violinesque arpeggio pattern where you play a higher note in the arpeggio then go back to the next lower chord tone, playing through the shape. That same pattern continues throughout the entire climb.

The next eight measures of the solo (bars 25 to 32) contain a variety of metal soloing techniques. The first four bars of this section start with some pentatonic play. In bar 27, use a two-notes-per-string, fast, alternate-picked pattern. Play down the pentatonic scale in two groups of three strings, then a group of two strings. In bar 28, there's a fast-picked two-string bit, where I change the top note each time, adding in the flat 5 (G♯) from the D blues scale. That kind of two-notes-per-string alternate picking has a real aggressive sound to it, when played fast. (String crossing on a down stroke each time adds to that.) It's also a completely different type of right-hand technique, as opposed to the double picking and sweep picking that's appeared previously in the solo. In bars 29 and 30, there's a repeating scale pattern in seconds. Then, on the climb at the end of this section (bars 31 and 32), there's a very classically influenced lick that's a bit more difficult to execute. This idea requires sweep picking through the small arpeggio shape, then playing a line from the scale right after the arpeggio. This is heavily influenced by one of my all-time favorite players and heroes, Ritchie Blackmore.

The last eight bars of the solo are a combination of two- and three-string arpeggios. The two-bar two-string/three-string pattern is just repeated through bars 33 to 38. The only thing that changes is the arpeggio shape. The pick strokes are all notated, so please pay strict attention to them, as it'll help you play everything more efficiently. On the climb in the final two bars, there's another two-string arpeggio sequence—this time, in a slightly different two-string sweep sixteenth-note pattern.

There are many metal techniques covered in this solo—plenty to improve your technique and expand your solo vocabulary.

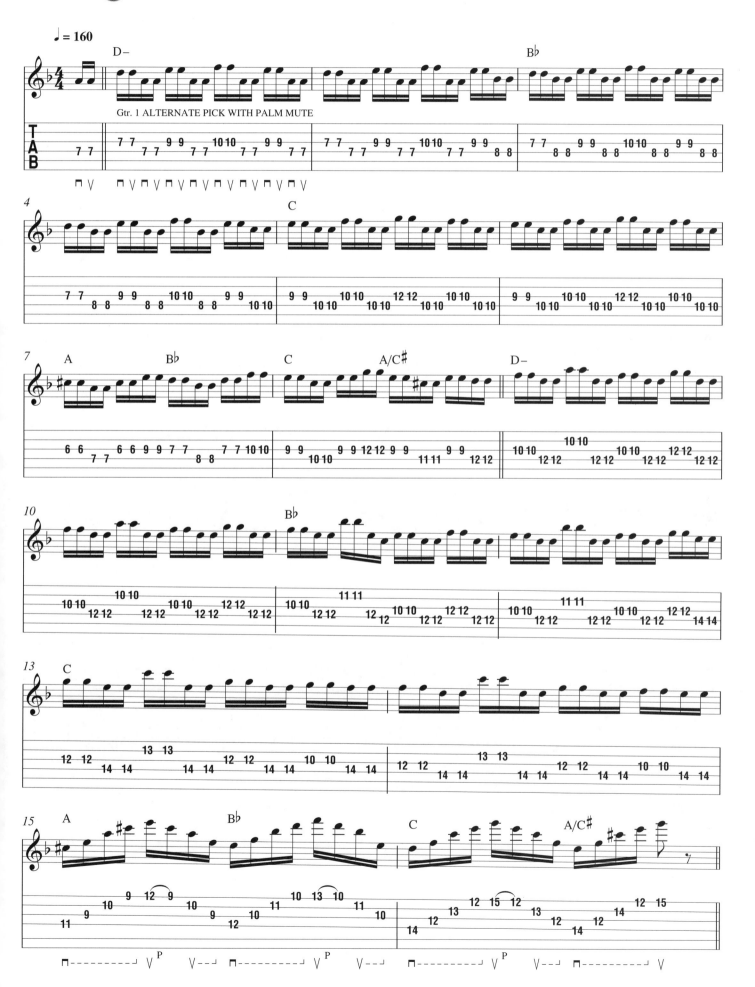

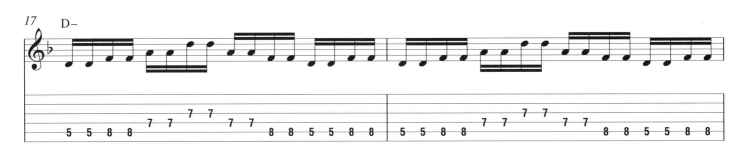

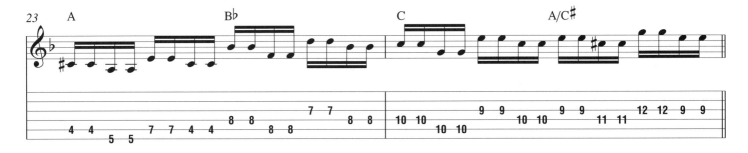

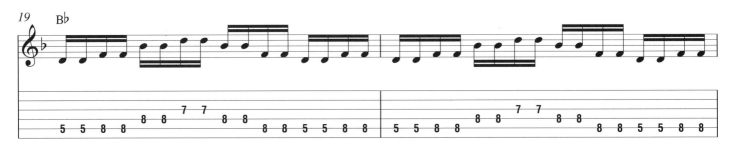

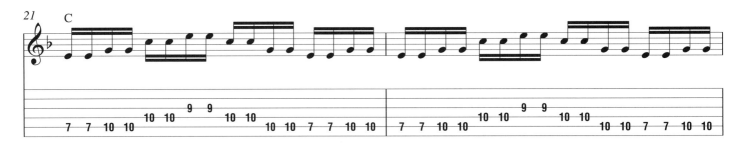

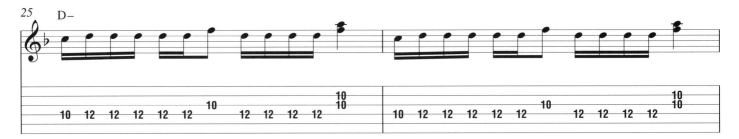

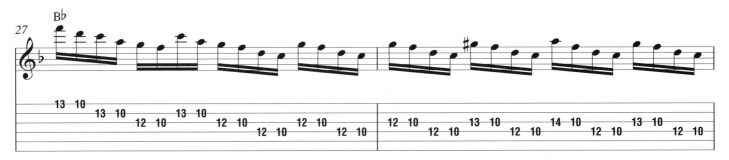

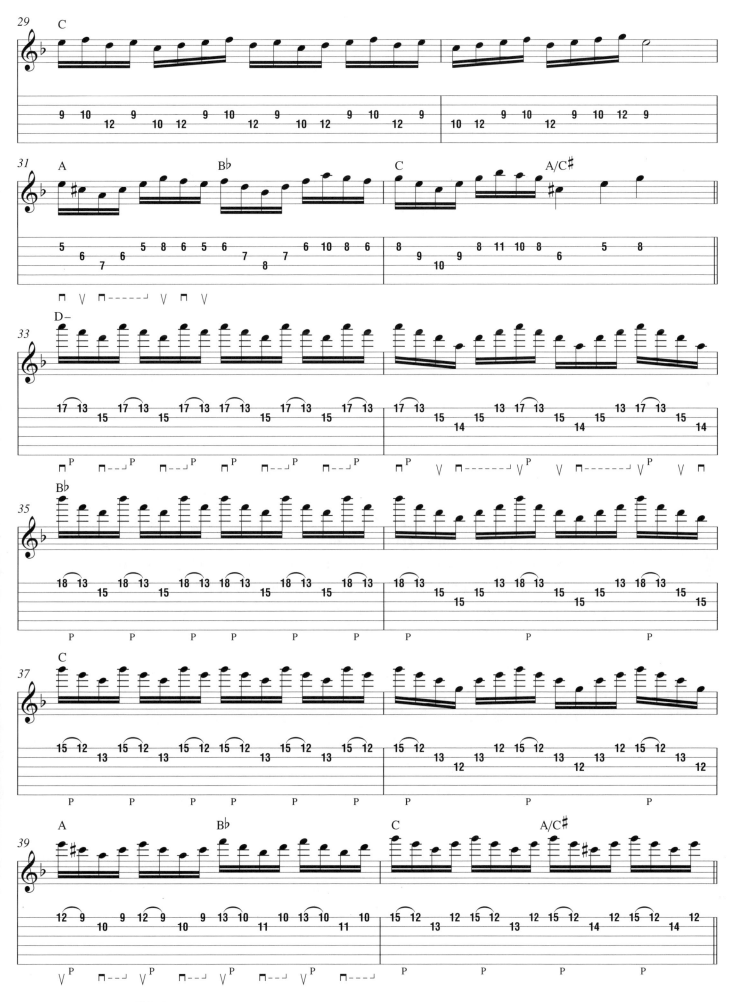

FIG. 3.2. "European Metal Double-Picking Etude," Solo Section

CHAPTER 4

Diatonic Scale Patterns and Melodic Sequences

In this chapter, we'll discuss diatonic scale patterns. I've mentioned these several times in earlier chapters, and now, I'll go into more detail, as these are quite useful on many different levels. *Diatonic* just means within the scale; you're just plugging a numerical pattern into the scale. These patterns are great for building technical command, as well as creating melodies and solo ideas. This chapter illustrates them in a more exercise-like fashion. In chapter 5, there will be some solo-context examples.

An easy way to understand these patterns is to think of each degree of the scale as a number, with 1 being the tonic/scale root and 8 being the octave. Then, just plug in each numerical sequence.

One commonly used and very musical diatonic scale pattern is playing the scale in a four-note sequence, 1-2-3-4, then going to the second note in the scale, playing 2-3-4-5, then the third tone 3-4-5-6, and so on. Then descend, playing the pattern in reverse: 8-7-6-5, 7-6-5-4, 6-5-4-3, etc.

Figure 4.1 is a small one-octave four-note sequence in A natural minor, using sixteenth notes. It turns around at the octave and is very conducive to being played in a circle. In the first two examples, I show the scale pattern in only a one-octave scale shape. This makes it quicker to internalize and easier to play, since less string crossing is involved.

Practice these patterns in any scale, any key, and any fingering type you like. I advise you to play them in the scales that you use and with fingerings you're relatively comfortable with. They are written here in various natural and harmonic minor scale fingerings, because those are scales I primarily use in my own playing.

FIG. 4.1. Four-Note Sequence in A Natural Minor

Figure 4.2 is once again the four-note sequence. However, this time, it's in the harmonic-minor scale, and instead of even sixteenth notes, it's played in triplets. Once again, it's a one-octave shape, but the triplet rhythm makes it a bit trickier to recognize the sequence. One of the cool things about these patterns is that, in addition to playing them in various scales, you can also play them using different rhythmic note values. The triplet rhythm almost makes the fours sound like a different melodic sequence. Varying the rhythm like this is great for executing the patterns over different grooves at varying speeds.

FIG. 4.2. Four-Note Sequence in A Harmonic Minor with Triplets

Figure 4.3 is back in A natural minor. This time, I'm showing it across a full two-octave scale shape. I practice this in a combination of two A minor fingerings: the three-note-per-string shape, and then, in the higher register and in-position fingering. This works great for me, but as I've mentioned previously, you can cross the strings with the sequence in any fingering or combination of fingerings you like. After I hit the second octave, I skip up two scale tones and then descend. I do this so the pattern turns around evenly in a circle, which is great for that aerobic type of technical practice.

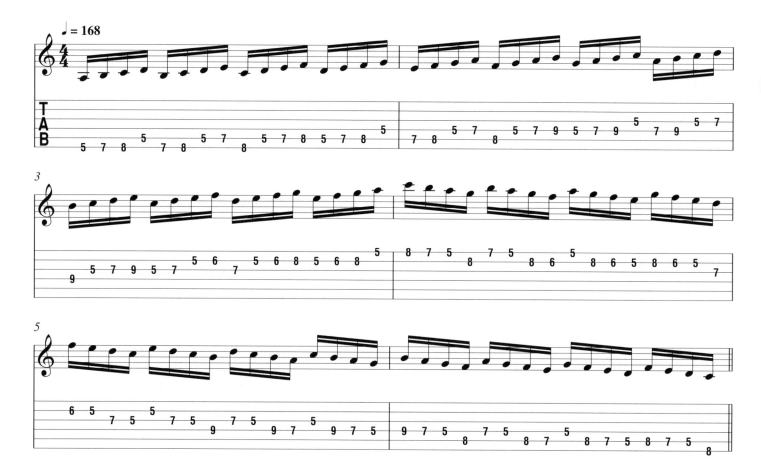

FIG. 4.3. Four-Note Sequence in A Natural Minor: Two Octaves

Figure 4.4, like figure 4.2, is in A harmonic minor and in triplets. This time, just like figure 4.3, it's played in two octaves. I use the identical combination of fingering types, as in figure 4.3 (except changing one note to make it harmonic minor), and turn the pattern around the same way (skipping to the note a third away after hitting the tonic in the second octave). The bigger scale shape and increased string crossing make these two examples considerably more difficult to work up, tempo-wise.

FIG. 4.4. Four-Note Sequence in A Harmonic Minor with Triplets: Two Octaves

Figure 4.5 is once again the "fours" sequence. The key is now E harmonic minor. This time, it's played across the strings in one scale position, then played down a single string that connects to another position of the scale. Playing and practicing these in varying combinations—across the strings, as well as up and down the neck, on single strings—makes them quite useful as soloing tools.

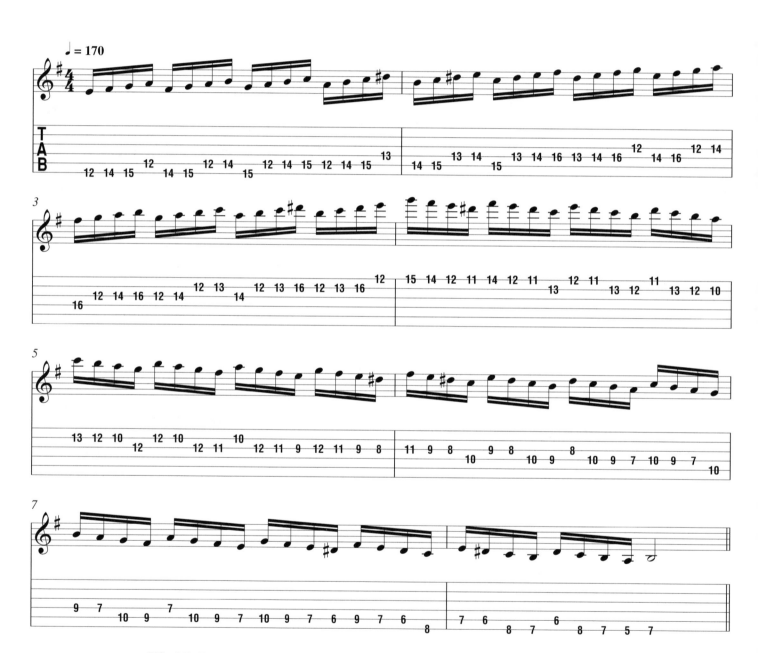

FIG. 4.5. Four-Note Sequence in E Harmonic Minor with Varying Scale Positions

Figure 4.6 is a new diatonic scale pattern, playing the scale in what's known as *thirds*, which means playing the scale tone and then playing a note a diatonic third (two scale degrees) away. The numerical pattern would be 1-3, 2-4, 3-5, 4-6, 5-7, etc., and then descending, the pattern repeats in reverse. Here, it is in triplets, but it works great in varying rhythms as well.

FIG. 4.6. Diatonic Scale Pattern in Three-Note Triplets

Figure 4.7 is another triplet-based pattern playing the scale by moving approximately three notes at a time. This example is in harmonic minor, and I've added a small harmonic minor line at both turnaround points to connect it in a circle.

A good way to practice all of these is by playing them at a challenging speed but one that you're completely in control of, in continuous fashion. You can navigate them in the same key through different fingerings or play the same fingering moving through various keys. Varying note values and playing them at different speeds really helps your command, synchronization, and control.

FIG. 4.7. A Harmonic Minor Scale Pattern

Figure 4.8 is another new scale pattern, playing the scale in what I call *seconds*; you play a scale tone, then its next lower scale tone (while ascending). The pattern numerically would be 2-1, 3-2, 4-3, 5-4, 6-5, 7-6, etc. When descending, play a note in the scale, then its next higher scale tone (7-8, 6-7, 5-6, 4-5, etc.). A good way to see all these patterns is by playing them in a one-octave scale, on a single string. This one is in B harmonic minor, in sixteenth notes.

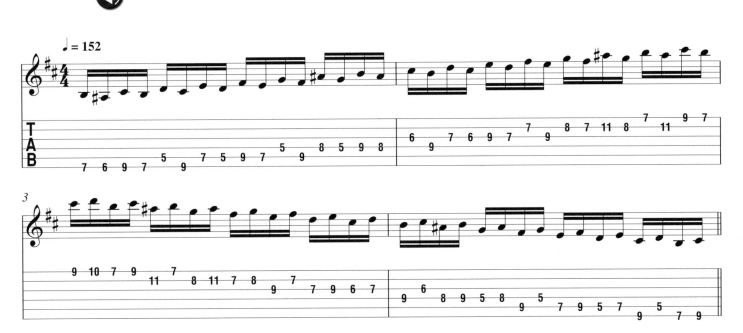

FIG. 4.8. B Harmonic Minor Scale Pattern in Seconds

In figure 4.9, we're back to the four-note pattern in sixteenth notes. This time, however, it's played up and down the neck on a single string. This is a great pattern that will help with alternate-picking speed. Navigating it on a single string can be somewhat tricky, at first. But since there's no string crossing involved, it's quite easy to alternate pick, once you gain control of the single-string thing.

This example is in A natural minor, but it's helpful to practice it in different scales and keys. You can also play this one on different strings, as seeing the scale on a single string is obviously a useful bit of guitar knowledge.

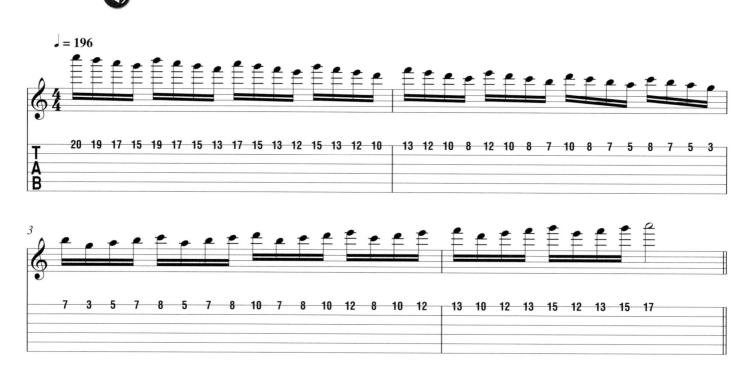

FIG. 4.9. Four-Note Scale Pattern on a Single String

CHAPTER 5

Solo Context Licks and Melodic Sequences

In chapter 4, we discussed diatonic scale patterns in more of an exercise/technique–building type of way. In my opinion, this is the easiest way to understand them and to get them under your hands. Now, we'll look at some examples that involve using them as more of a soloing tool.

In figure 5.1, the four-note sequence is primarily in B natural minor. However, in measure 3 on the climb and in measure 5, I add the leading tone A♯ from the B harmonic minor scale. I start out playing the pattern across the strings, then on a single string, moving up the neck. Once I get to the high B at the 19th fret, I descend on a single string and then resolve it using a very cool classically influenced arpeggio, the B minor triad with the second degree of the scale (C♯) added in.

This lick makes for a great practice pattern, as well as a soloing idea. It's helpful to play this type of pattern (fours moving in a combination of across the strings and up and down the neck) in multiple scales and keys. The trickiest part of the lick is the quick turnaround at the top, which will take some practice when trying to execute it at faster speeds.

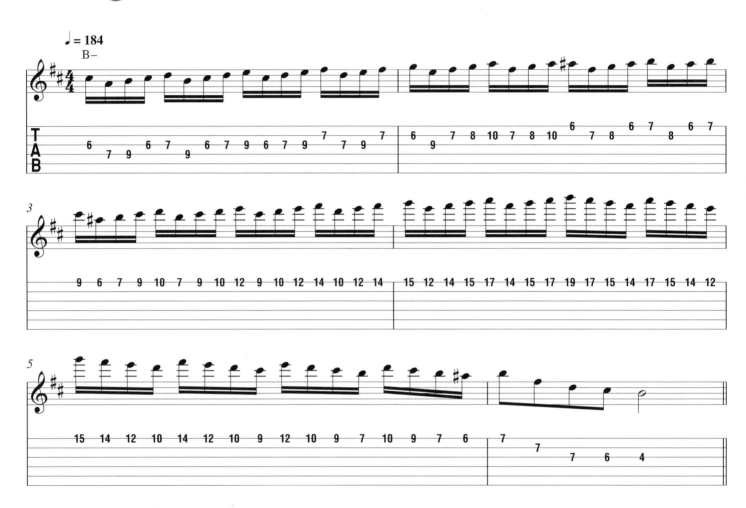

FIG. 5.1. Four-Note Sequence in B Natural/Harmonic Minor

Figure 5.2 is another example with the four-note pattern in sixteenth notes, this time using the E harmonic minor scale. This example is in two-measure phrases where I start the four-note climb on each chord tone of the E minor triad. In the first two measures, it starts and ends on the tonic E. Then in measures 3 and 4, it starts and resolves on the 3rd of the chord, G, and in measures 5 and 6, the 5th of the chord, B. This is an effective way to bring out the sound of the chord you're soloing over, and it also displays a different sequential idea of the four-note pattern (starting on a chord tone as opposed to playing it straight up or down the scale). At the end of the lick in measure 7, there's a run in what's known as *mixed minor*: there are notes from both the natural and harmonic minor scales, in the ascending run. This type of run is heavily inspired by classical violin, as well as by two of my heroes and main guitar influences: Yngwie Malmsteen and Uli Jon Roth.

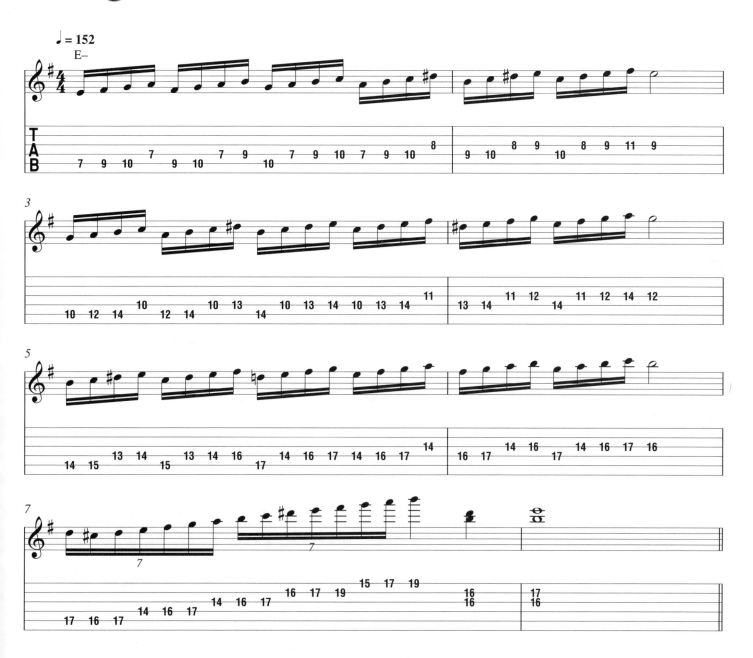

FIG. 5.2. Four-Note Sequence in E Harmonic Minor

In figure 5.3, the four-note pattern is within sixteenth-note triplets (sextuplets), played across the B natural minor scale. Along with the four-note pattern, I mix in a two-string ascending lick involving hammer-ons and pull-offs (beats 3 and 4 of measure 2, and again in measure 4). I use this pattern quite a bit in my soloing, and it works well moving either across the strings or up and down the neck on sets of strings. I finish the run on a two-string, six-note climb on the top two strings resolving to the tonic, B.

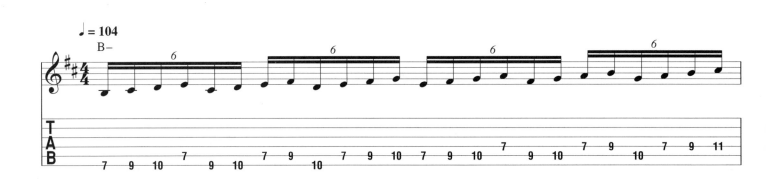

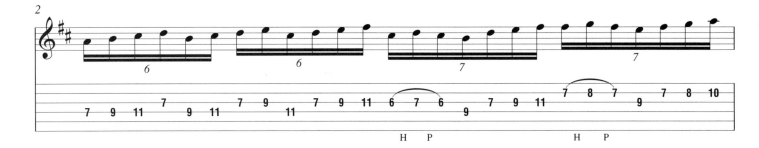

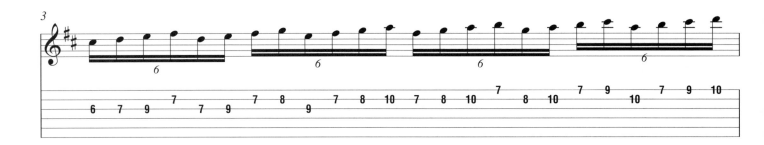

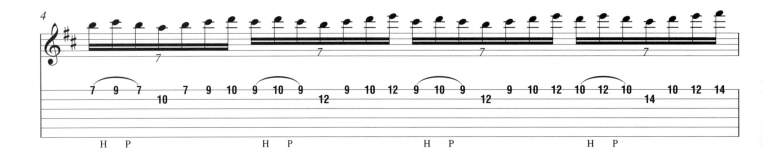

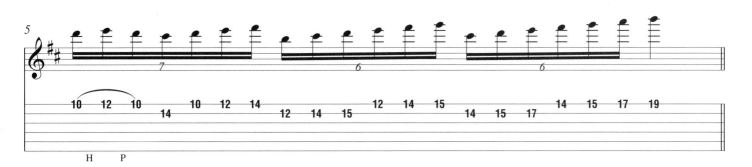

FIG. 5.3. Four-Note Pattern in Triplets

Figure 5.4 is a very effective variation of the four-note sequence, instead of ascending or descending straight in fours, the first lower tone of the four-note group is repeated. The pattern is in A harmonic minor and involves even sixteenth notes, but there are only three pitches. This works great for single-string solo play but can also be played across the strings. I'll use this pattern at varying speeds, as it has a nice melodic aspect to it and works equally well, whether it's a high octane double-bass metal bit or a nice melodic medium tempo/slow ballad section, that you're soloing over. In the first two measures, I'm playing the pattern and sequencing it in intervals of thirds. Then in measures 3 and 4, it goes to a straight single-string four-note climb before resolving. The single-string aspect of the lick makes it easy to alternate pick. Navigating the jump in thirds on a single string will certainly help your facility for playing up and down the neck.

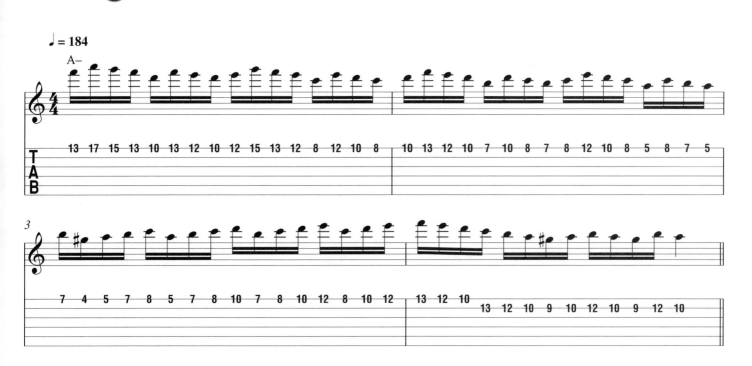

FIG. 5.4. Four-Note Sequence Variation in A Harmonic Minor

Figure 5.5 is just a fast descending neo-classical lick straight down the E Phrygian dominant scale (the very commonly used fifth mode of harmonic minor), in seconds. This one is all alternate picked and displays the pattern nicely in combinations of across the strings as well as down the neck. A cool practice bit is to take a lick like this (or any of these other patterns, as well) and to try and work out your own sequences using various sets of strings and single-string combinations. In addition to helping your chops, it'll also help your knowledge of the fretboard.

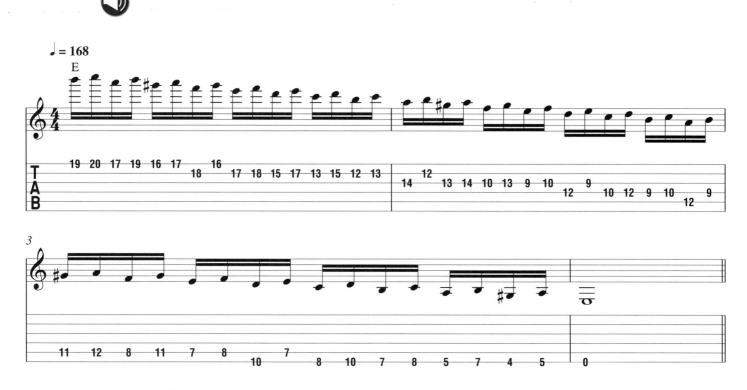

FIG. 5.5. Neo-Classical Lick in E Phrygian Dominant

Figure 5.6 is a run using the thirds pattern in a combination of B natural and harmonic minor. The lick is sequenced by starting the pattern on varying scale degrees. In the first two beats, I play straight down in thirds, then in beat 3, I go back to the next lower scale tone and then play the thirds pattern. A similar motif is used in the second measure before heading straight down the harmonic minor scale using the pattern and then resolving it. I've used this idea in various solos of mine, as it works great at many different tempos over a variety of metal/hard rock grooves.

FIG. 5.6. B Mixed-Minor Run Using Pattern in Thirds

Figure 5.7 is a lick once again using the E Phrygian dominant scale—again, a favorite and frequently used scale of mine. I'm playing down the scale in groups of threes, sequencing the pattern at first on two strings. Then, in combination with some snakey, Eastern-sounding harmonic minor motifs, I take the pattern across the strings and down the neck. This is another run inspired by Yngwie Malmsteen and Uli Jon Roth. The utilization of hammer-ons and pull-offs really adds to the fluid sound of the lick.

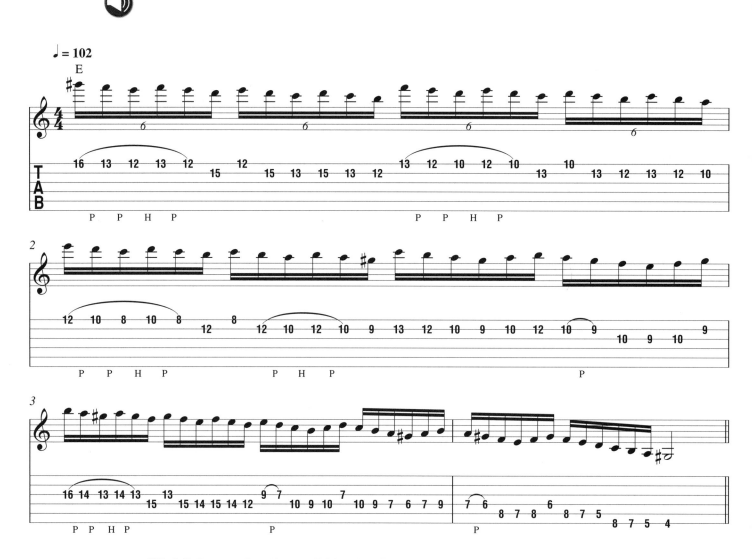

FIG. 5.7. Descending Lick on E Phrygian Dominant

Figure 5.8 is another classically influenced run using the A harmonic minor scale. In the first two measures, I play straight up the scale in groups of three notes. Then in measures 3 and 4, it's just the same run an octave higher. In measure 5, I descend using the three-note pattern straight down the scale. In the last three measures, I change up, descending in fours but still maintaining the triplet rhythm.

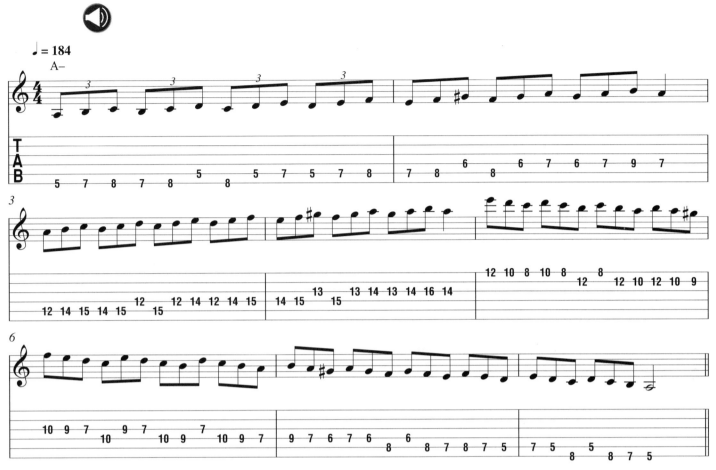

FIG. 5.8. Neo-Classical Run in A Harmonic Minor

Figure 5.9 is a small section of the track "Blackmore's Boogie" from my record *Virtuosic Vendetta.* It's a Baroque sounding run (inspired by both J.S. Bach and Ritchie Blackmore) that is a combination of first playing up the G minor scale in fours and then descending using the thirds pattern. The use of the D major two-string arpeggio in measure 4 is borrowed from the G harmonic minor scale and resolves the lick nicely.

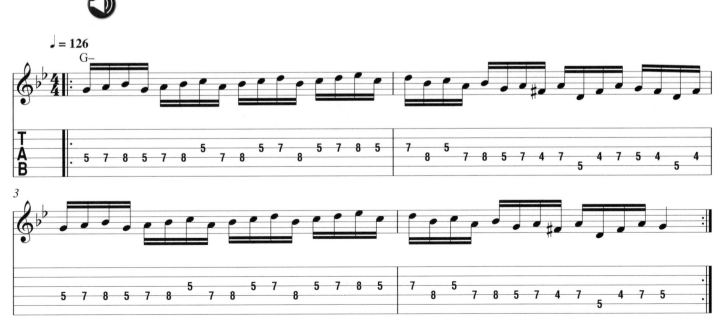

FIG. 5.9. "Blackmore's Boogie" Excerpt

Figure 5.10, the final example of this chapter, is another neo-classical solo idea, and once again, in the E Phrygian dominant scale. I'm using the seconds pattern, this time in triplets.

In the first measure, I descend straight down the scale in seconds, and then combine that with a classically influenced harmonic minor motif. In the next two measures, it's just the same exact thing, an octave lower. Playing in octaves is a very effective way of stretching a lick along, giving you increased fretboard knowledge and command. Plus, if the run sounds cool in one octave, it'll be even cooler in multiple octaves. Measure 5 repeats the first measure two octaves lower. Then, an ascending G♯ diminished seventh arpeggio combined with a descending scale run finishes out the example.

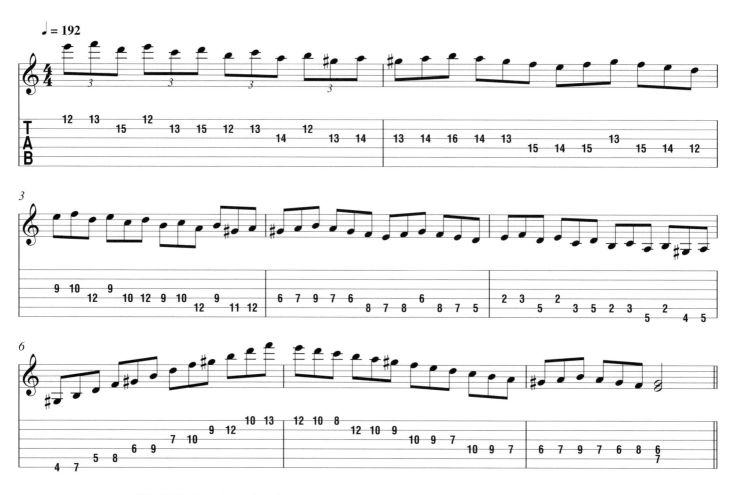

FIG. 5.10. Neo-Classical Run in Seconds

CHAPTER 6

"Neo-Classical Shredfest Number 3"

"Neo-Classical Shredfest Number 3" is a classically influenced etude I composed years ago, inspired by Bach's sonatas and partitas for violin. My thinking was to take some of those ideas and motifs, make them more guitar friendly, and create something that would combine diatonic scale patterns along with classically influenced lines and arpeggios. The entire piece is in triplets, so it's a great way to help strengthen executing that particular note value at a fast tempo, as well as recognizing the various melodic ideas played in the context of a piece.

The first section is in the key of F♯ harmonic minor. It is based predominantly around playing the scale in a three-note pattern. In bar 1, I ascend three notes at a time, then in bar 2, follow with a melodic harmonic minor motif. Bar 3 repeats the first bar. Bar 4 has a motif similar to bar 2 but just moving up the scale. Bars 5 and 6 are the same as the first two bars, but played an octave higher. And then in bar 7 (first ending), there's a descending three-note scale pattern before heading down the scale.

It's very important, when playing a piece, to recognize the various patterns and motifs and how the piece is put together. This helps you internalize the piece faster and gives you a better understanding of the ideas used.

The first six bars then repeat, and in the second ending, I'm descending in fours within the scale but in triplets rhythmically. I start on D then descend in the four-note scale pattern for that bar. In the following bar, I start a tritone lower (on G♯) with another bar of triplet-based descending fours. Bar 11 repeats bar 9 an octave lower and then goes into an ascending diminished run to finish off that section.

Section 2 changes key to A minor. I'm using a combination of natural and harmonic minor in this section.

In addition to practicing this track in entire sections, it's helpful to play it in four- and eight-bar pieces as well. In the first four bars of the second section (measures 13–16), I'm playing the scale in intervals of thirds. In bar 13, it's the natural minor scale in thirds starting and ending on the tonic A. Then in the next bar, the thirds ascending pattern is once again repeated, just starting and ending on D within the A minor scale. Notice the classical V to I resolution in the first three bars of this section, as the scale patterns follow suit nicely with the chords. In bar 15, the thirds pattern is played once again, this time starting and ending on G. A short harmonic minor lick follows to complete the last bar of this first four-bar excerpt.

In the next four bars, I switch to a different diatonic scale pattern, this time playing down the scale in seconds. Since all these patterns have been covered previously, they should be easier to recognize by now. In bar 17, I start on B and descend in seconds. Then in bar 18, I start a third away, on G, and descend in seconds. In bars 19 and 20, I start, once again, a third away from the previous bar's starting note, and this time, continue all the way down the scale using the seconds pattern.

The next four bars (measures 21–24) involve a violin-influenced three-octave A minor arpeggio utilizing sweep picking. After the full three-octave shape, I then descend with another violin-influenced pattern, playing one chord tone of the arpeggio, then going to the next higher chord tone and then back again in a three-note pattern, all the way down the arpeggio shape—a very cool and effective motif. This four-bar section makes a challenging practice bit on its own.

In measures 25 and 26, I use a four-string, two-octave harmonic minor run (just ascending straight up the scale three notes per string in a four-string shape repeated in two octaves). For these types of runs, I use economy picking, but it can be alternate picked as well. Then in measures 27 and 28, I use a five-string A minor arpeggio shape played with a combination of sweep and alternate picking. The entire section ends with a descending three-note run in bar 29 followed by a previously used harmonic minor motif in bar 30. In bar 31, it's back to the descending thirds and ends with a small one-octave A minor arpeggio in the last two beats of measure 32.

The third section (at measure 33) of the "Shredfest" is quite short: only eight bars, and all two-string arpeggios played utilizing sweep picking. (Pay strict attention to the pick strokes noted.) All the arpeggios are on strings 3 and 4, and all start with the root of the arpeggio—a very classically influenced chord sequence utilizing the diatonic arpeggios from both A natural and harmonic minor, along with a few two-string diminished shapes used to connect everything with a chromatic ascending bass motion. Once again, this eight-bar section also makes a great practice study and can be used to help develop your two-string sweeping technique.

The fourth and final section of the "Shredfest" (starting measure 41) is based on a picking pattern covered previously, playing the scale in an alternate-picked doubled-up three-note pattern. It starts in a combination of A natural and harmonic minor, and then later on, modulates to D. I'm utilizing a variety of Baroque type motifs in this entire fourth section.

The first eight measures of this section are played entirely on the second string. I begin by starting on the set of tones containing the raised 7th (or "leading tone," as it's also known), then up to the next higher set of scale tones; each time, it returns to the set containing the leading tone before resolving it in bar 2 of the second ending (measure 46). In the next seven measures (measures 47–53), it's once again the scale in fours. It's in triplets, this time, played down the top two strings diatonically with a classical single-string lick in bar 53 in between, before it again resolves. The last eight measures (measures 55–62) change key to D minor (once again the natural/harmonic minor combination). Then, it's back to the alternate-picked doubled-up three-note pattern. I play the pattern on a set of strings (strings 3 and 4). That lower string to higher string diatonic movement creates the very Baroque sounding harmonic movement. It moves down strings 3 and 4 within the scale. In the final two bars it's back to the fours in triplets before resolving to the new tonic, D.

Memorizing and executing the entire "Neoclassical Shredfest Number 3" at tempo is quite an undertaking. Once again, I encourage you to practice it in individual sections as well as four- and eight-measure increments. Isolating the various ideas and moving them to different keys/string set combinations will help you learn to create your own licks.

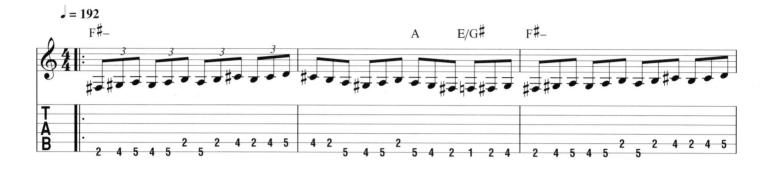

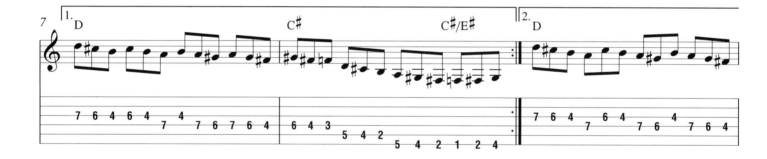

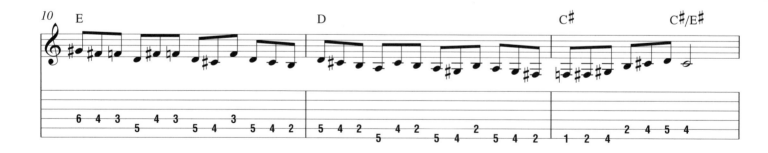

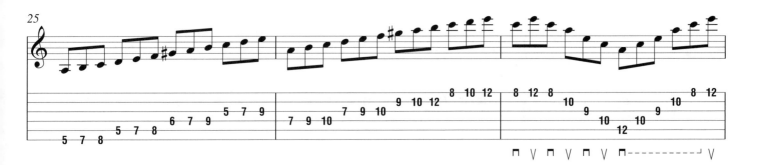

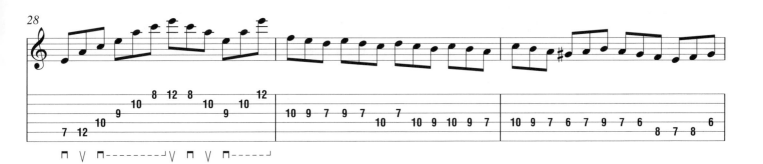

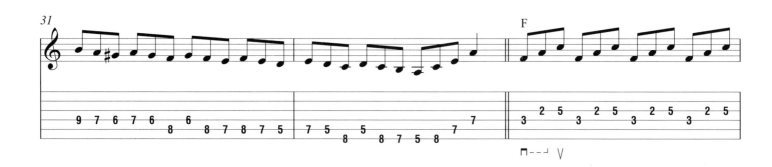

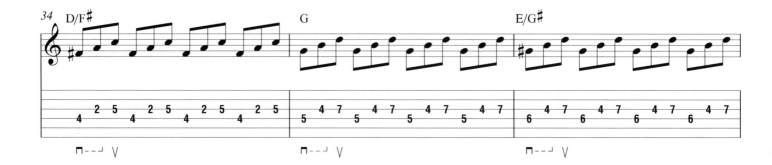

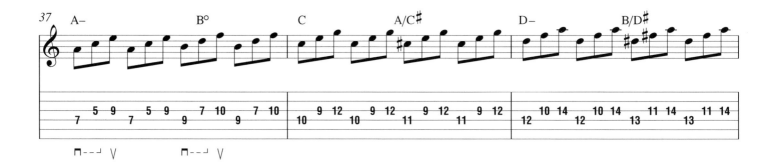

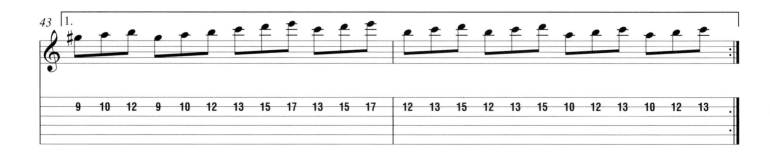

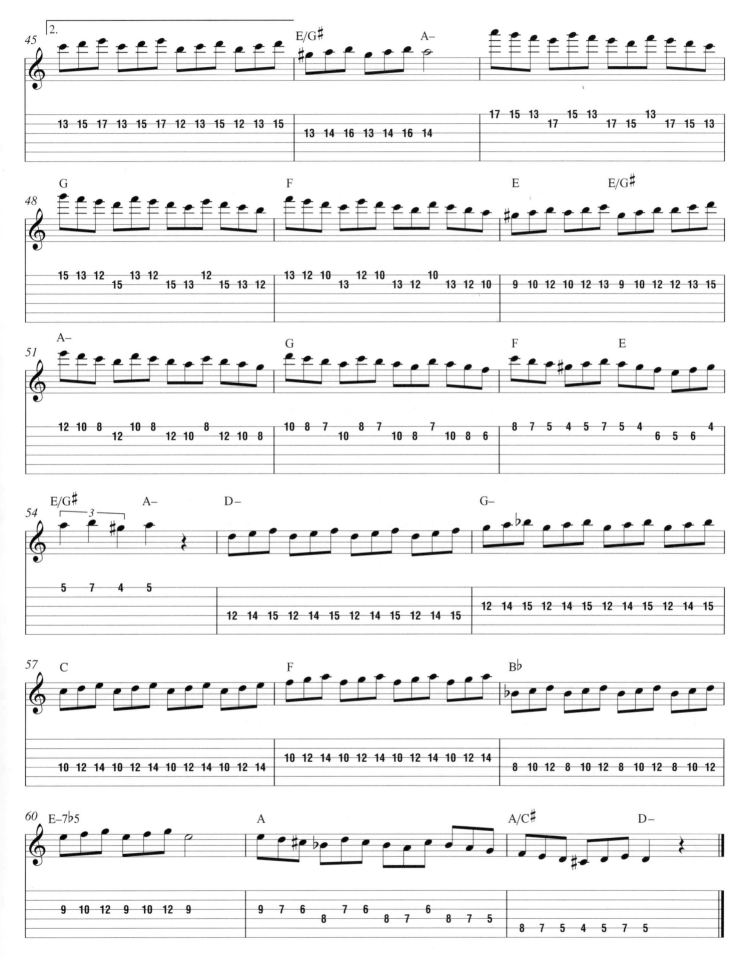

FIG. 6.1. "Neo-Classical Shredfest Number 3"

CHAPTER 7

Alternate Picking Scale Fragments and Picking Sequences

I mentioned scale fragments several times in previous chapters. In this chapter, I'll go into much greater detail on how to use scale fragments as a great way to develop and improve your picking technique, as well as how they're a very effective soloing tool.

Once again, a *scale fragment* is a piece of a scale, which we can play in a circular/repetitive pattern. (Some are more melodic than others.) The idea is to take a fairly short fragment (usually one to three beats, though some scale fragments can be one or two measures long), move it around diatonically to create longer solo ideas/sequences, and also, use it to improve the synchronization between your picking and fretting hands. The fact that it's short in length makes it fairly easy to memorize. Once you can execute it cleanly in one area, moving it across the strings and up/down the neck is the next step. Some scale fragments are on a single string. Most commonly, they're on a set of strings (strings 1 and 2, or strings 3 and 4, for example)—sometimes even three or four strings.

This chapter is in two sections. The first set of scale fragments/scale fragment soloing ideas are all based on eighth- or sixteenth-note triplets. In the second half, they're mostly straight/even sixteenth-note figures. Note: It's also very common to marry/connect several different scale fragments of the same rhythmic value, combining them to make longer more interesting soloing ideas.

PART 1. TRIPLET-FEEL FRAGMENTS

Figure 7.1 is a melodic two-bar scale fragment that I like to use. The first two beats are a single-string idea that I'm playing at a fast tempo (quarter note = 196). I also use this one at varying tempos as a sixteenth-note triplet. I use a short melodic phrase to finish the first measure. In the next measure, it's just the scale in the diatonic four-note sequence, played in triplets on a set of two strings.

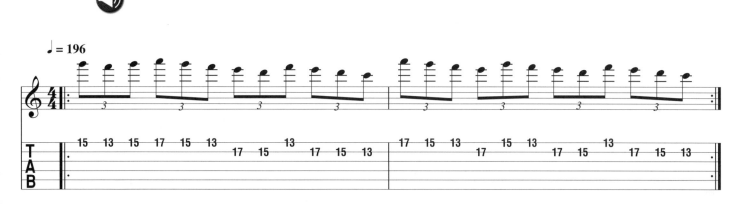

FIG. 7.1. Two-Bar Melodic Scale Fragment

Figure 7.2 is a pair of six-note single-string fragments. The second sextuplet is the same fragment as shown in figure 7.1, beats 1 and 2. Its more common variation is on the first beat of figure 7.2. Since you start each sextuplet on a down stroke and end on an up, the lick is very easy to move around. When you cross a string or go to another set of tones inside the scale, you're always automatically starting on a down stroke, making it a no-brainer to alternate pick. Also, it's great to isolate single-string ideas like this one on each of the six strings, in varying registers of the neck. Just take one (or both of the six-note figures, and play it on a specific string continuously). Your pick reacts differently on your high E as opposed to your G string, as opposed to your A string, as well as the different areas of the neck.

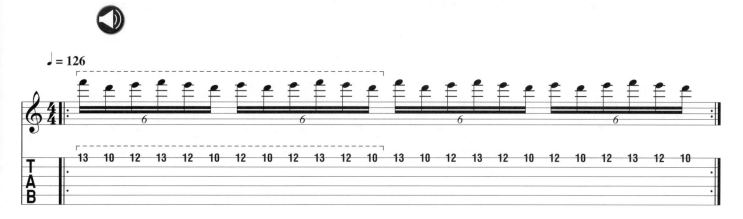

FIG. 7.2. Sextuplet Fragment

Figure 7.3 goes back to chapter 1, where I used this fragment not only to help build technique but to internalize those speed/three-notes-per-string scales. In beat 1, you have three notes on one string and one note on the top string. While crossing over, be sure that you attack the top string with an upstroke, thus continuing the alternate-picking pattern. This fragment is also used in chapter 8's "Neo-Classical String-Skipping Etude." Beat 2 of figure 7.3 is just six notes ascending. This example is really just a simple combination of two one-beat scale fragments married to each other to form a slightly longer lick.

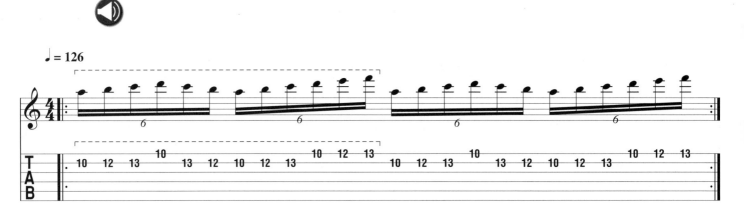

FIG. 7.3. Sextuplet Combo Fragment

Figure 7.4 is a two-bar lick in harmonic minor, which combines the fragments from fragment 7.3 with a short, melodic scale idea (which appears in beat 3 of the first bar). Combining any of the fragments with simple melodic phrasing motifs helps you stretch the ideas further, as well as makes it more interesting/melodic and less exercise-like.

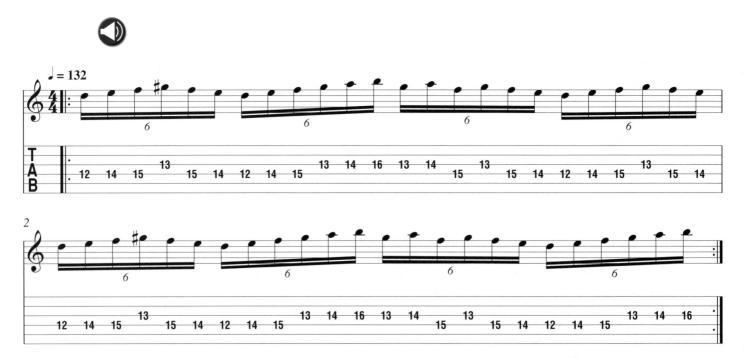

FIG. 7.4. Harmonic Minor Lick with Melodic Fragment

The fragment in figure 7.5 is once again in harmonic minor, similar to figure 7.4. Beat 1 has the single-string fragment from figure 7.2, followed by a short melodic idea (descending down the scale in two groups of three notes). That melodic fragment connects to the second half of this lick, which is the two-beat fragment from figure 7.3. This is an example showing how smaller fragments combined with a short melodic idea can create a longer/cooler lick. Again, practice these examples in various tonalities and on different string sets.

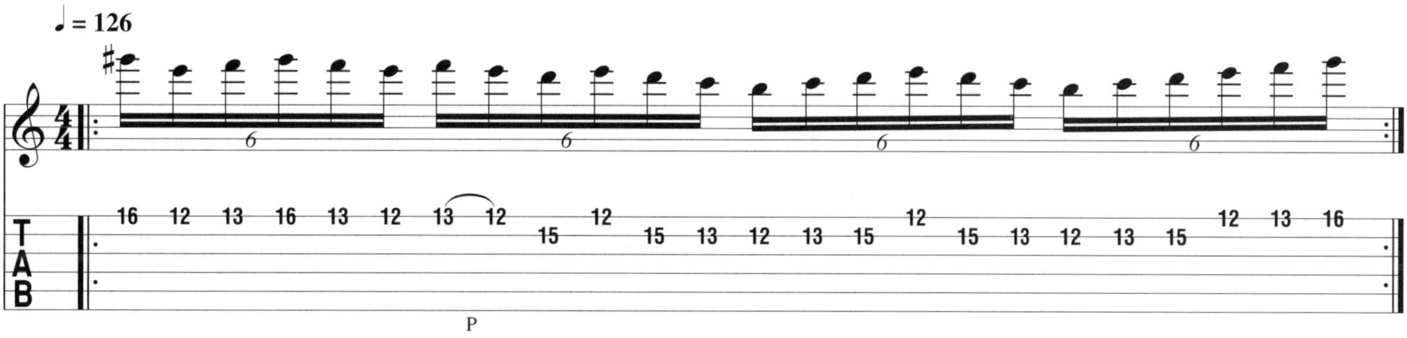

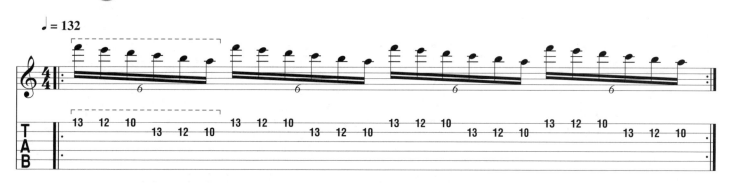

FIG. 7.5. A Harmonic Minor Sextuplet Fragment

Figure 7.6 is just six notes descending. This one-beat fragment is commonly used by many players. It can easily be stretched in quite a few combinations across the strings, up and down the neck.

FIG. 7.6. Six Notes Descending Fragment

Figure 7.7 follows suit with fragments 7.4 and 7.5. Once again, a harmonic minor lick combines previously featured fragments with a short melodic motif.

FIG. 7.7. Harmonic Minor Combination Fragment

Solo Licks: Triplet Feel

In this next section, we will use the fragment examples to form longer solo licks.

Figure 7.8 is a diatonic exercise. The two-bar fragment from figure 7.1 moves up the neck diatonically on the top two strings, in E natural minor. I switch to E harmonic minor in the final four bars, and finish the sequence with a classically influenced line that resolves it. The drum groove clearly indicates how it sounds in context. This lick also works great to warm up. Moving the two-bar idea up and down the neck, on varying string sets, and in different keys, helps both synchronization and fretboard knowledge.

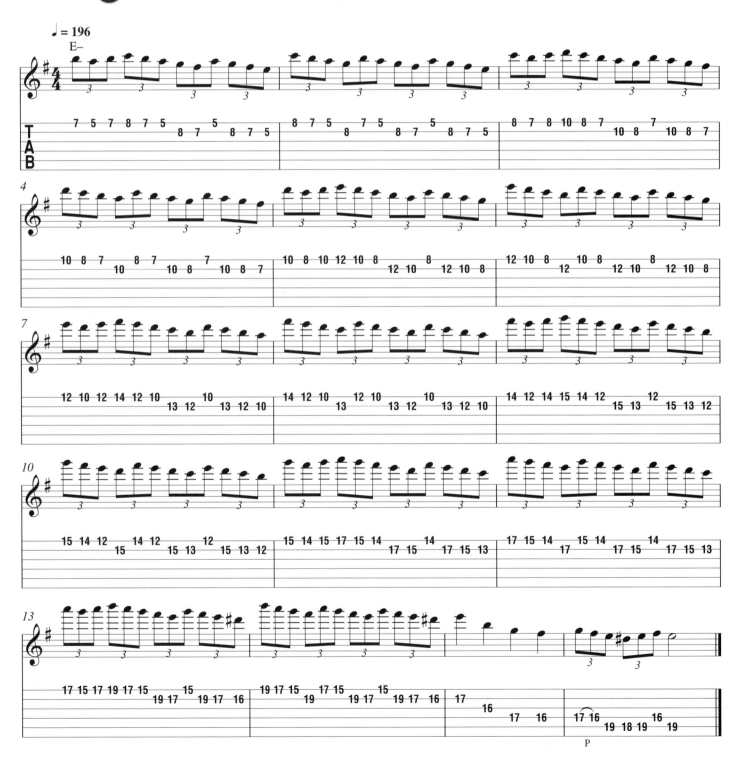

FIG. 7.8. Diatonic Exercise

In figure 7.9, I'm using fragment 7.2, moving it down the neck once again in E minor. This two-string sequence gives you a classical sounding resolution as you move it down the neck. I finish the lick with an octave-jumping string skip in E harmonic minor.

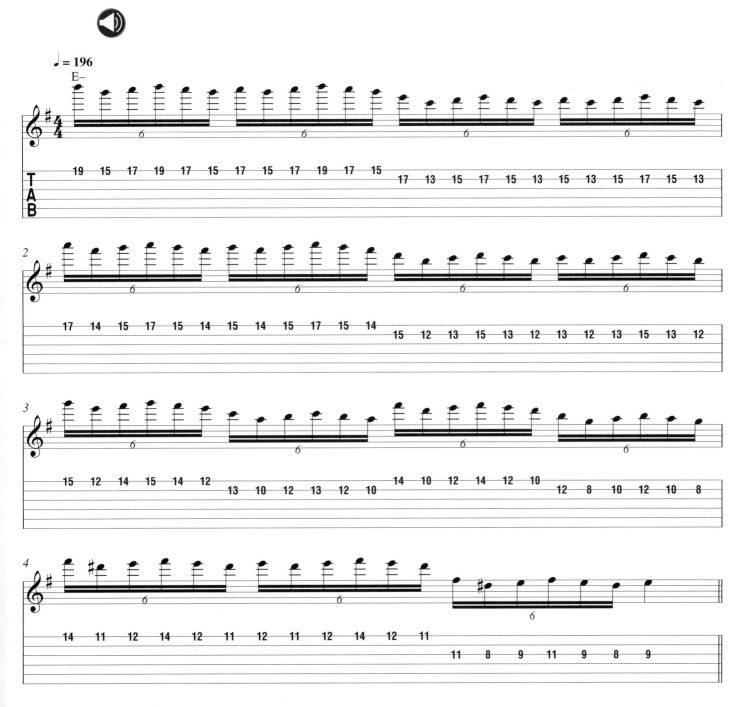

FIG. 7.9. Two-String Lick

Figure 7.10 features the same fragment again. This time, I'm using a classical motif where I target each chord tone of the E minor triad. The middle note of each fragment, as well as beats 2 and 4 of the first two bars, outlines the triad: first the root, then the third of the chord G, after that the fifth B, and finally, back to the tonic E an octave higher. I move the pattern up the scale in bar 3 (still with the chord tone as the middle note) and then finish up on a high bend up to the tonic. Very effective, cool sounding, neo-classical motif.

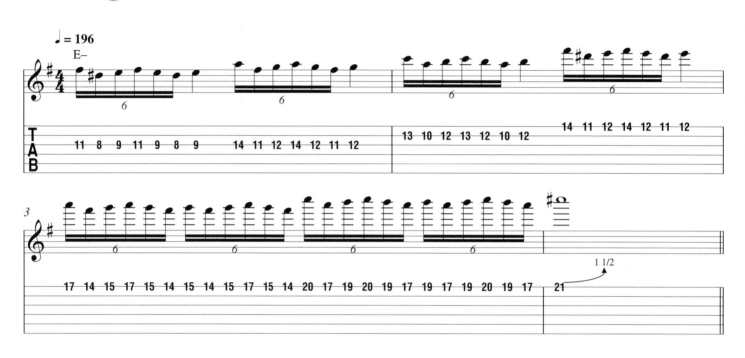

FIG. 7.10. Neo-Classical Lick

Figure 7.11 is quite easy to internalize, as I'm using two previously featured fragments. In the first two bars, it's just the combination of scale fragment 7.3 with a four-string scale run. (I used this same pattern in the first chapter with the speed scales, so it should be quite familiar to you by now.) I'm in A harmonic minor, and bar 2 is exactly the same as the first bar, just an octave higher. In the second half of the lick, I take the fragment from 7.2 and move it down a symmetrical harmonic-minor scale shape in three octaves. This is a prime example of how playing ideas in multiple octaves really enables you to stretch them further.

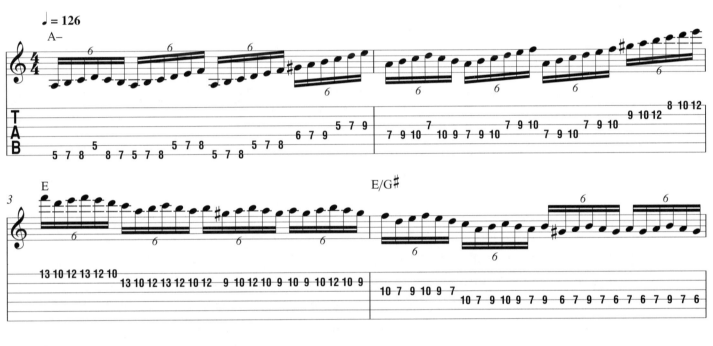

FIG. 7.11. Combo Lick

While figure 7.8 was more of a diatonic exercise, 7.12 is much more of a solo context idea, utilizing the fragment from 7.1. This lick is in the fifth mode of A harmonic minor, which is E dominant Phrygian. I combine the fragment in 7.1 with melodic, classically influenced harmonic-minor motifs to help construct the lick. Bars 5 and 6 are identical to the first two bars, just played in a different area of the scale. Bar 7 is the same as bar 3, just an octave lower. In the last bar, the lick resolves to the tonic of the scale.

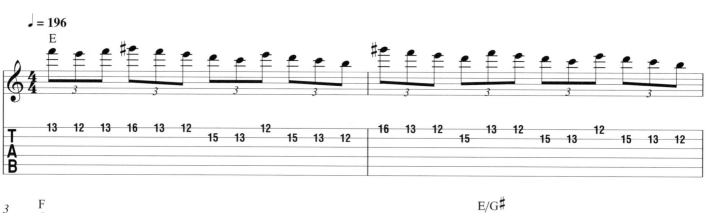

FIG. 7.12. Soloistic Lick

Lick example 7.13 combines fragment examples 7.4 and 7.6. This lick is in B natural minor; in bars 1 and 2, I plug fragment 7.4 into a six-note two-octave shape. I combine the fragment with a six-note two-octave run, and then repeat the same exact idea an octave higher in bars 3 and 4. This six-tone shape (known sometimes as a hexatonic scale) can help outline and imply various scales and modes. I use them frequently in my playing. In this case, it's just the first six tones from B minor.

These hexatonic shapes work extremely well. Playing them fast across the strings is much easier than a straight-up diatonic scale fingering, since there's only one combination of fret-hand spacing involved. The second part of lick 7.13 (bars 5 and 6) is just fragment 6 first played down the scale on two strings then across the strings before resolving.

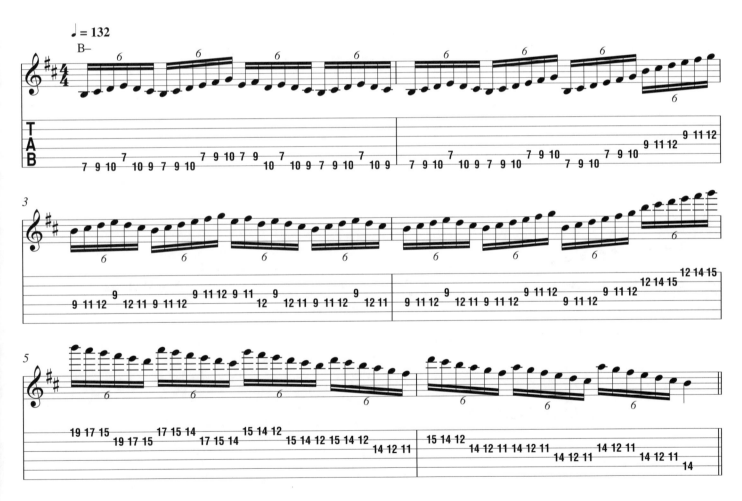

FIG. 7.13. Hexatonic Lick

Lick example 7.14, again in E dominant Phrygian, uses fragment example 7.7. I combine fragment example 7.7 with a hexatonic multi-octave scale run. This harmonic minor hexatonic outlines a diminished 7 arpeggio. I use this shape in harmonic minor/Phrygian dominant all the time, as it sounds killer and it's easy to play fast up and down the neck. The rest of lick 7.14 is a melodic classically influenced motif I used on quite a few previously covered examples, played down the neck in a symmetrical harmonic-minor shape.

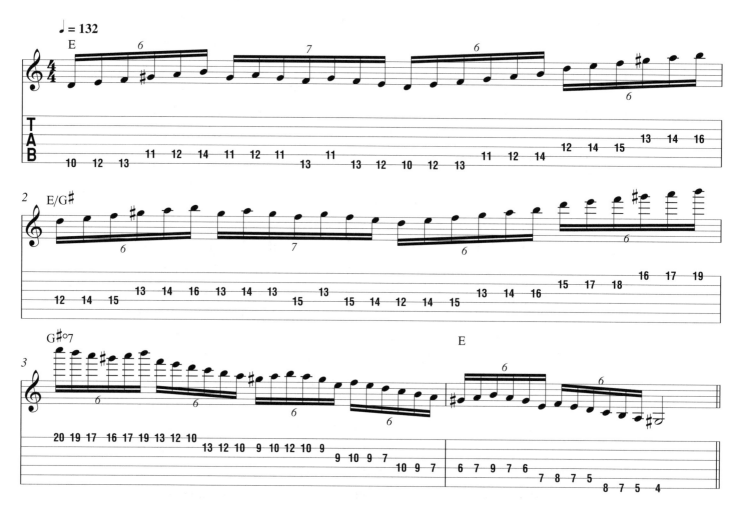

FIG. 7.14. Multi-Octave Lick

Lick example 7.15 is straight out of chapter 1 where I combine the double up picking pattern and a scale run. In chapter 1, it's played straight across the A natural minor scale, and in much more of an exercise/drill type of format. Here, it's more of a solo idea, as it's played first in a four-string, two-octave run (first twelve tones/four strings of the scale in two octaves, a cool/effective scale shape I like to use). Then, the double-up pattern continues moving up the neck in A minor on the top two strings. The lick finishes up with the combination of a two-string diatonic climb. The last half of figure 7.15 then ends with the bend up to the tonic.

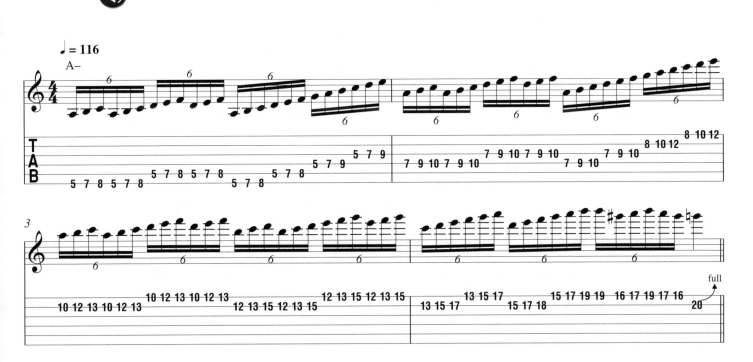

FIG. 7.15. Four-String Lick

You might find lick example 7.16 a bit more difficult than some of the previous examples. While it sounds pretty crazy, all I'm doing is plugging scale fragment examples 7.4 and 7.5 into a string skipping diminished 7 arpeggio. A good way to practice this lick is to first memorize it as is, and then try and put it into an easier left-hand shape. After mastering the picking pattern, move it back to the more difficult diminished-string skip. You can see by the lick examples that I plug all of these fragment ideas into a variety of tonalities and left-hand shapes.

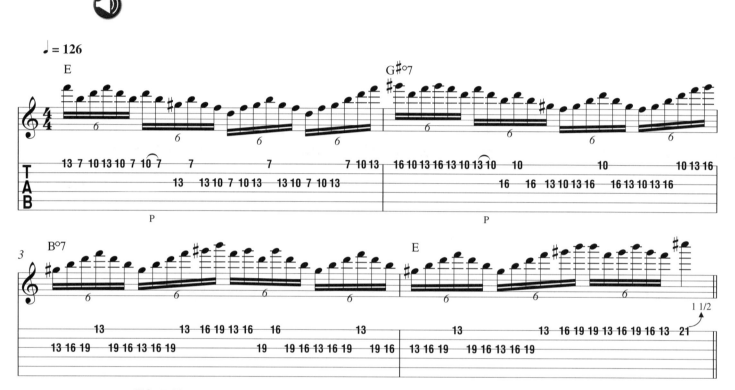

FIG. 7.16. String Skipping Lick

PART 2. SIXTEENTH-FEEL FRAGMENTS

In part 2, all of my scale fragment examples and solo-context licks are even sixteenth-note based patterns, with the exception of a few examples containing quintuplets/five-note groupings. While I do employ a combination of economy and alternate picking on all of these licks/fragments, most players would play them all alternate-picked.

Fragment 7.17 is a single-string fragment that's only two beats long. It's in A harmonic minor, and since I'm turning the fragment around on the leading tone, it's got a cool/dramatic sound to it. Once again, since there's no string crossing involved, single-string fragments are easier to work up tempo-wise, and a great way to help build speed and synchronization. Practice this fragment in any scale or key, on any string. It works especially well sequenced down the neck on a single string.

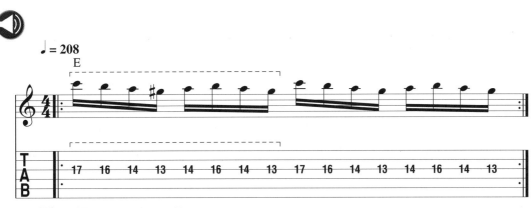

FIG. 7.17. Single-String Fragment

Fragment 7.18 is a short, one-beat lick that I swiped from Romantic era violin virtuoso Niccolò Paganini. Once again in A harmonic minor, it's got a dark/dramatic sound to it. I often use this one in combination with fragment 7.17, as they work great together.

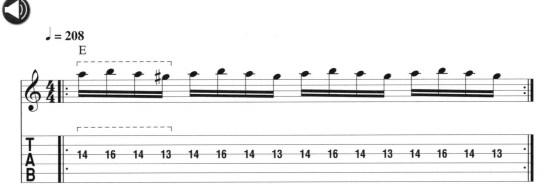

FIG. 7.18. Paganini Fragment

Fragment 7.19 is a five-note grouping or quintuplet. It's a very simple lick, just one string set, three notes per string, played in a circle. Many players find odd groupings tough to execute in time. One main reason for this is the fact that they sound much more awkward when played at a slower speed. Of course, you want to practice this at a speed where you can execute it cleanly, but it's not a bad idea to up the tempo, as it might give you an idea of how the five-note grouping will flow at a faster, less awkward speed. This one moves quite easily up and down the neck on any string set, as well as across the strings.

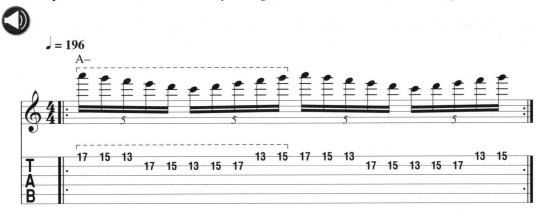

FIG. 7.19. Quintuplet Grouping Fragment

Fragment 7.20 is a picking pattern I've been playing since I was a teenager. This lick stems from Al Di Meola, whom I consider the godfather of ultra-fast guitar. He was blazing up these scale runs and fast picked fragments back in the late '70s, long before anyone heard the term "shred," and I was just blown away when I heard him. The lick, which I call "4s in a circle," starts by descending down the scale in three sets of four notes (diatonic four-note pattern covered in chapter 4). Then it turns around in a circle, with one set of ascending fours. You can see that even though it's only one measure long, it's quite a bit of work for your pick hand.

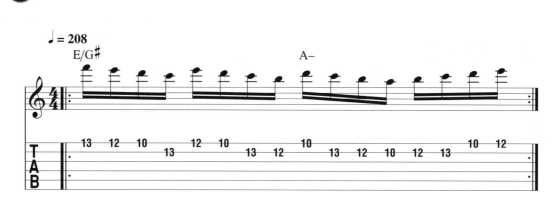

FIG. 7.20. 4s in a Circle

Solo Licks: Sixteenth Feel

Fragment 7.21 is another one-measure circular lick in A harmonic minor/E Phrygian Dominant. I often try to come up with circular picking patterns that make for a great practice drill as well as sound cool, melodic in a solo context. I've been playing this one for quite a while and use it frequently. Not a ton of string crossing, so you might find this one easy to work up tempo-wise.

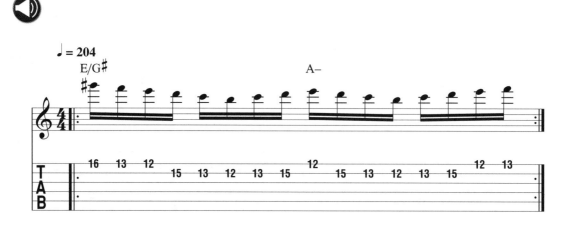

FIG. 7.21. One-Measure Circular Lick

Fragment 7.22 is a three-beat variation of the 4s in a circle pattern (figure 7.20). Once again, it's quite a bit of work for your pick-hand in a lick that's only three beats long.

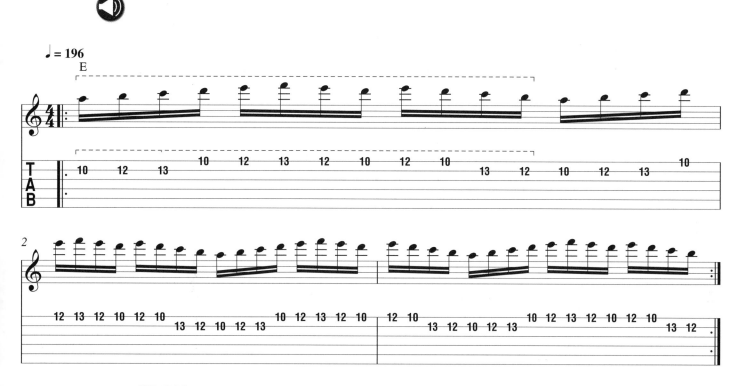

FIG. 7.22. Three-Beat Variation

Fragment 7.23 started out as another one of those circular picking drills discussed previously. A cool practice bit is to take this three-string, two-measure pattern, and play it diatonically up or down the neck on a set of any three strings.

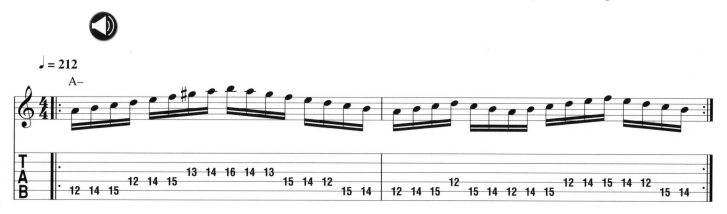

FIG. 7.23. Circular Picking Drill

Figure 7.24 is very much like some of the fragment examples in part 1 of this chapter, where I combine the scale fragment with a short melodic phrase to form a more interesting lick. In this one, it's just fragment 7.17 played an octave higher, with a short melodic phrase added to it to form yet another circular-picking pattern.

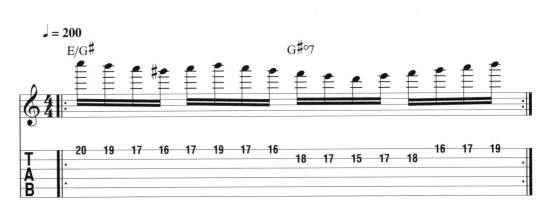

FIG. 7.24. Circular Picking Pattern

Solo example 7.25 is in E Phrygian dominant. It starts out with fragment example 7.20 (the 4s in a circle pattern). I play that lick twice and then connect it to fragment example 7.21, which is also repeated. Then, I connect that back to fragment example 7.20 (4s in a circle pattern). This time, I'm playing that lick with only one note on the top string, so it might be a little tougher to execute with the additional string cross. After repeating the circular pattern, I continue down the scale in the diatonic four-note pattern before it resolves.

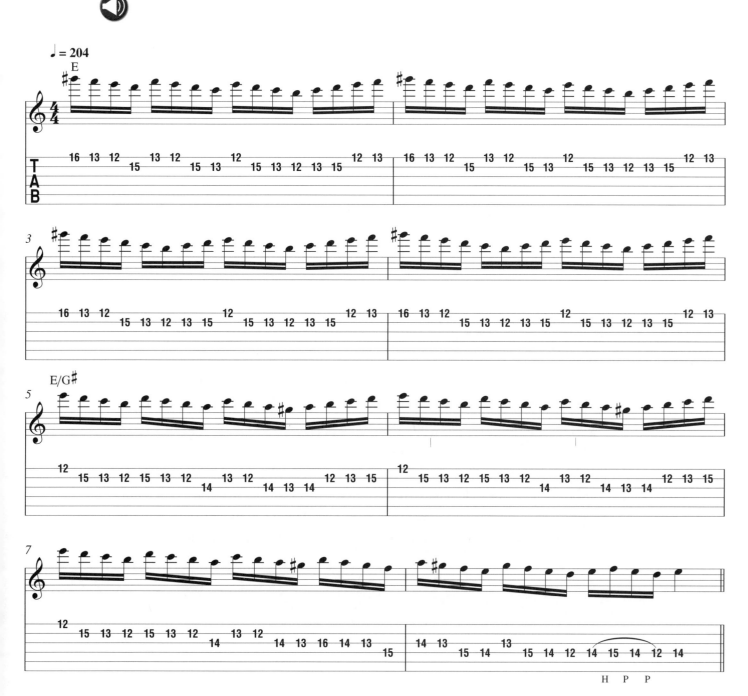

FIG. 7.25. Solo Example

Solo example 7.26 involves the quintuplet pattern in fragment 7.19. This one's in A natural minor, and I sequence the five-note grouping diatonically down the neck on strings 1 and 2. It finishes up with a three-note per string scale run in A minor across the strings.

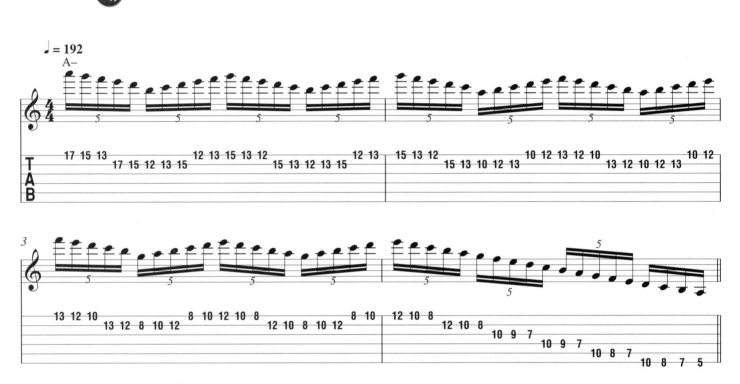

FIG. 7.26. Solo with Quintuplets

Solo example 7.27 is a cool/effective combination of several fragments. It starts out with fragment 7.24 played two times. After that, I play the very first fragment example three times (7.17) and connect that to fragment 7.19 (played twice). In measures 7 and 8, I play a combination of fragments 7.22 and 7.19. (Note: Fragment 7.22 is only three beats long. Since it's played twice and then connects to two-beat fragment 7.17 it makes a nice, even two-measure lick in itself). That entire two-measure phrase is then played again. The whole thing ends with a descending symmetrical harmonic minor run across the strings and down the neck.

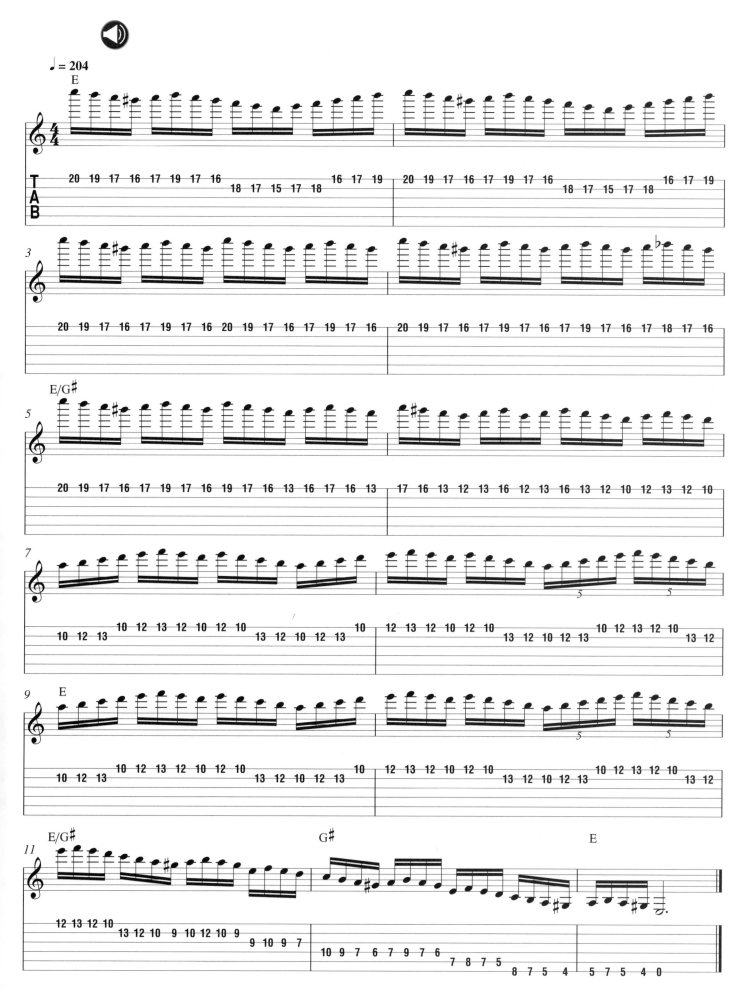

FIG. 7.27. Solo with a Combination of Fragments

In solo example 7.28, I take two-measure fragment 7.23 and move it up the neck in a combination of E natural and harmonic minor. After the diatonic climb, I ascend across the strings in E minor (bars 7 and 8). The last eight bars of the lick are once again fragment example 7.20 (4s in a circle lick). This time, I play that lick moving up the E minor scale, connecting the pattern on the top two strings. The lick then ends with the dramatic high bend up to the tonic. This one, along with solo context lick 7.27, are two of my favorites.

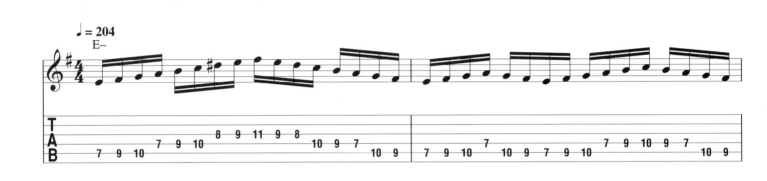

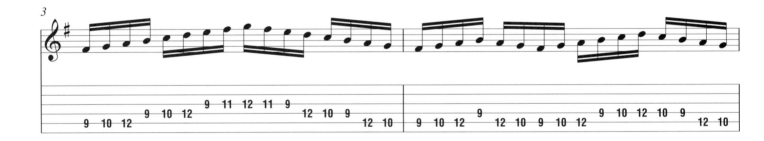

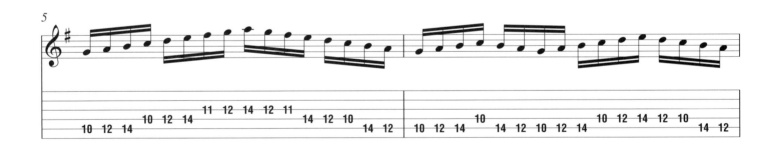

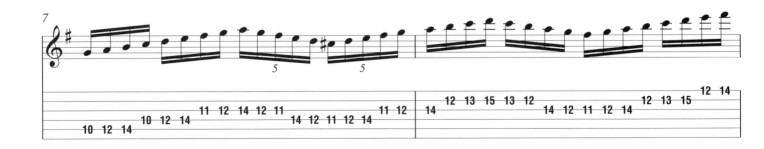

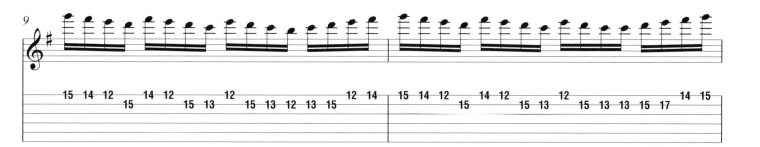

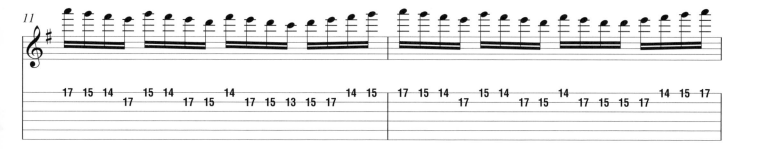

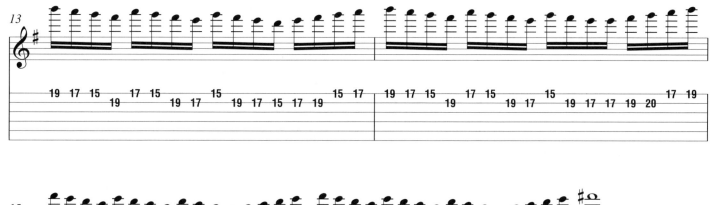

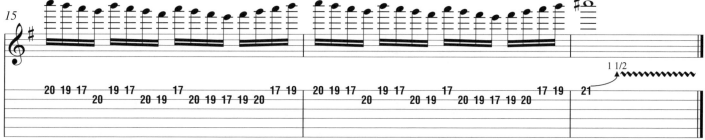

FIG. 7.28. Solo Lick Up the Neck

Lick example 7.29 is in B harmonic minor/F♯ Phrygian dominant. The scale shape I'm using is that four-string two-octave shape I often favor. This one works great in harmonic minor, as some of the fret-hand spacings of the scale can be tricky and awkward, and this shape works nicely. I play the ascending five-note pattern (fragment 7.19) across the four-string two-octave shape. In measures 5 and 6, I play the two-measure pattern contained in bars 7 and 8 of lick 7.27 (combination of fragments 6 and 3). In measure 7, it's back to lick 7.22. Then in the final measure, the lick ends with an Yngwie Malmsteen/Uli Jon Roth-inspired harmonic minor phrasing idea.

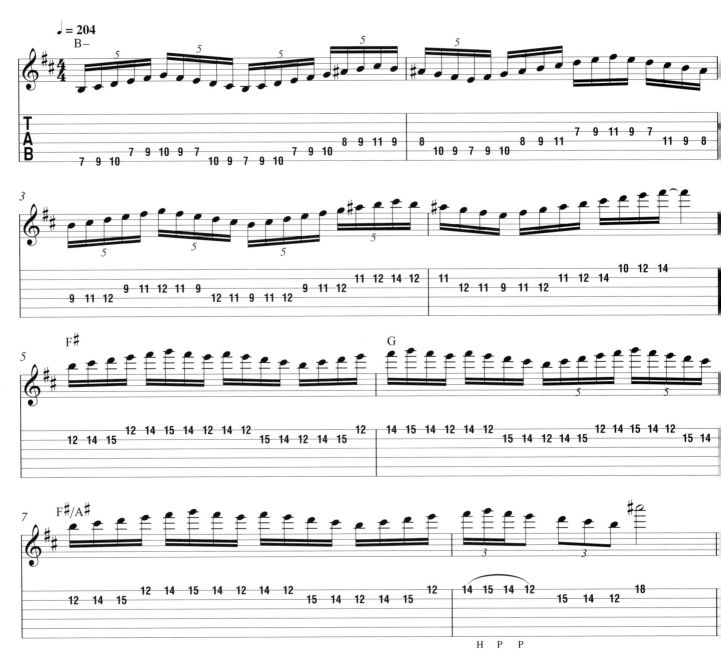

FIG. 7.29. Four-String, Two-Octave Shape in B Harmonic Minor

Quite a few picking patterns/fragments and solo context ideas are covered here. Practicing them will certainly help your pick hand technique and hopefully inspire you to create your own arsenal of blazing licks and fragments. One very effective way of coming up with new fragment ideas is to take an idea you've been executing at one particular note value (sixteenth triplets, for example), and then altering and creating a new variation using a different beat permutation (straight sixteenths, perhaps).

CHAPTER 8

"Neo-Classical String-Skipping Etude"

The "Neo-Classical String-Skipping Etude" will help you develop and improve your alternate picking. The study cycles through a very common Baroque chord sequence (A minor, D minor, G major, C major, F major, B diminished, E major), all diatonic to a combination of A natural and harmonic minor.

I play three tones on the fourth string, then each time, cross over to the next higher string, outlining the triadic chordal shape on the top three strings. If you keep this in mind, memorizing the etude will be much easier, as will recognizing these triad chord shapes. Start out on the fourth string with a down stroke, playing three tones, then cross over to the next higher string, always playing an upstroke, thus maintaining strict alternate picking. It's extremely important to pay strict attention to all the pick strokes notated.

The etude is sixteen bars long, but to start, I've broken it down into two easier-to-execute eight-bar sections. Each eight-bar excerpt will help you in playing the entire etude, and they're useful alternate-picking etudes on their own.

SECTION 1

In the first section, I'm doing away with any string skipping and just playing the first beat of each chord change four times. Here, it is just three notes on one string, one note on the next higher string, always crossing over on an upstroke (hence keeping the consistent alternate pattern). Since it's eight bars, as opposed to sixteen, and there's no string skipping, you'll automatically be able to play this section at a faster tempo and to control it easier; it's an excellent start to alternate picking when string crossing. The final run in bar 8 is known as a *mixed minor scale run*, a violin-influenced shape combining the natural and harmonic minor scales containing both 7th tones, G and G♯. I use economy picking (three notes per string, down/up/down, then down/up/down on the next string, etc.), but you can alternate-pick this run instead.

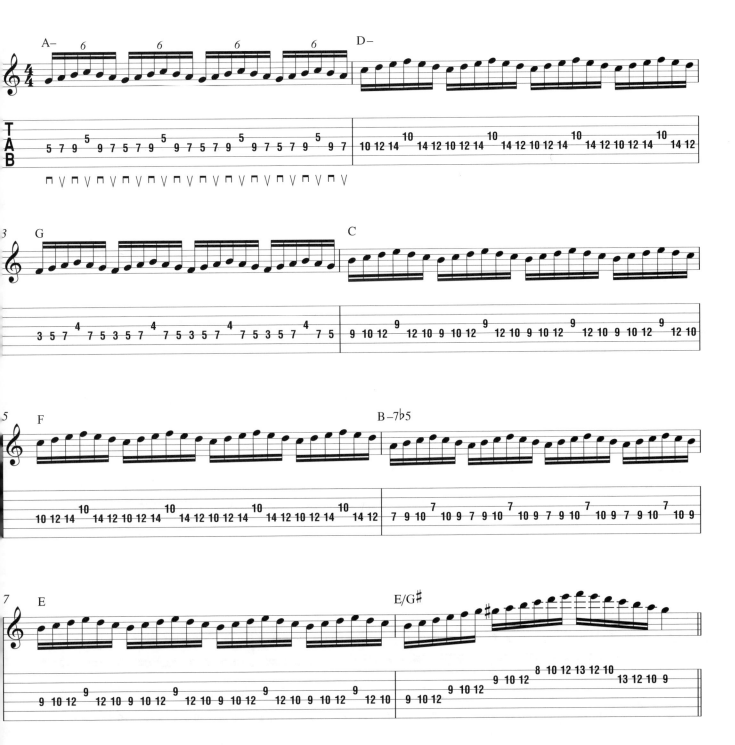

FIG. 8.1. "Neo-Classical String-Skipping Etude" Section 1

SECTION 2

Section 2 gets slightly more challenging, as in addition to the initial string cross of the first section, beat 2 of each measure includes a string skip. Once again, alternate picking remains constant throughout. You can see how this is a logical next step in trying to take on the full sixteen-bar etude. You can try each one of these sections individually or play them consecutively. You might find yourself executing each section at a faster speed on its own but then having to slow the tempo down a bit when combining them. Either way, all this makes for very good practice, as endurance is one excellent way to help build speed and technical command. This means playing things at a challenging speed that you're in control of, but for somewhat lengthy periods of time.

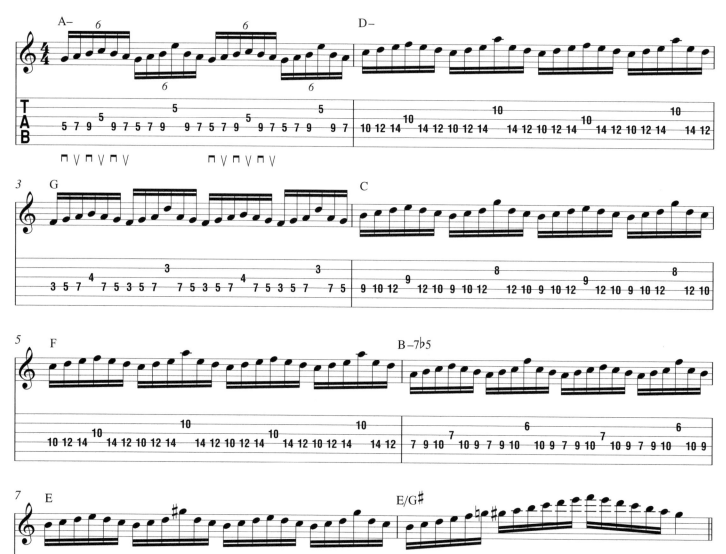

FIG. 8.2. "Neo-Classical String-Skipping Etude" Section 2

FULL SIXTEEN-BAR ETUDE

The entire etude employs one more string skip, this time skipping over two strings and outlining the full three-note chord shape. The triad shapes follow suit with the chord sequence, and the first three chords (A minor, D minor, G major) are just a one-bar phrase repeated. Then, in measures 7 through 10 (C major and F major), the motif changes up with a two-bar variation of the string-skipping pattern. Measures 11 and 12 outline the B diminished triad and return to the original one-bar pattern, while in bars 13 and 14 (E major), I use a two-bar variation once more.

The mixed minor run at the end is now a two-measure phrase and quite a bit more difficult to execute. Beat 3 of measure 15 includes a seven-note grouping where I'll slide into the additional note on the second string and then continue descending using alternate picking. In the last measure, there's another odd grouping: first, an eight-note grouping followed by a seven-note grouping. This is a run I use frequently and really think of more as a fifteen-note scale shape played over two beats. Make sure to hit the final target note G♯ on beat 3 of the measure; that should really help with playing the run in time.

Odd groupings can be tough in that you can't subdivide them and break them in half, so you'll have to work it up by practicing the run slowly with the metronome. The entire etude, as well as the two individual sections, should give you quite a few practice options.

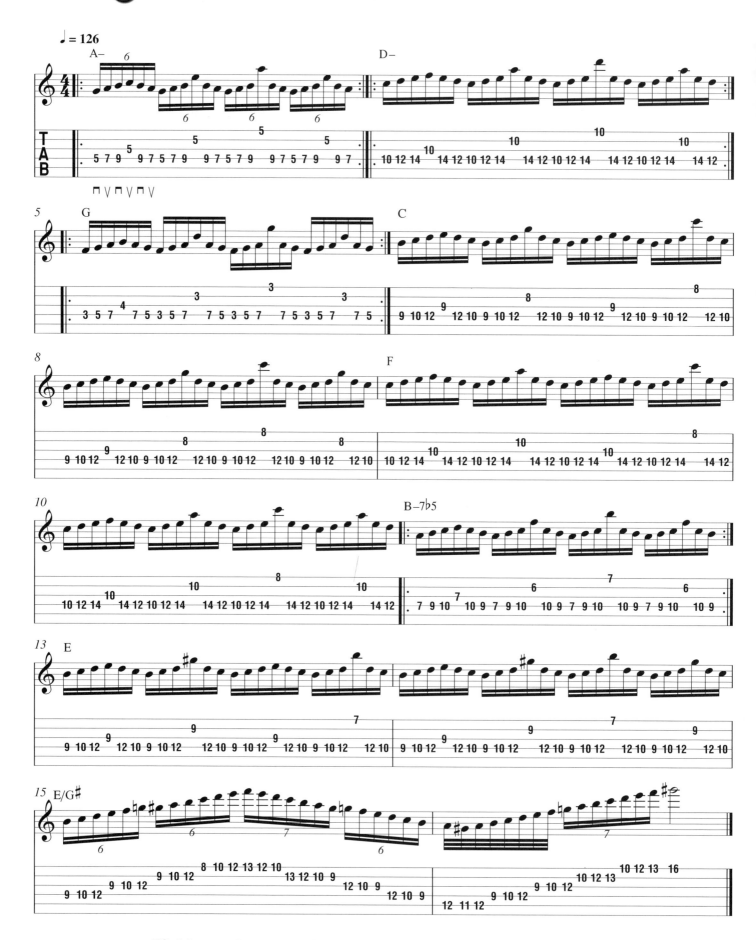

FIG. 8.3. "Neo-Classical String-Skipping Etude" Complete

CHAPTER 9

Open String Soloing Ideas/Motifs

In this chapter, I'll be talking about utilizing open strings for soloing ideas and melodic motifs. For decades now, open-string solo play has been a staple of just about every hard rock and metal player's vocabulary. The following examples will range from technique-building exercises to soloing licks and classically influenced melodic sections.

Figure 9.1 is a very simple exercise, using the E natural minor scale on the top string. I'm playing one note in the scale and then three open strings. I continue this pattern, moving up the scale as well as up the neck on my E string. This pattern is helpful for a variety of reasons. First off, since there's no string crossing, it's extremely easy to alternate pick and play at a relatively fast tempo. It also helps you to memorize the minor scale on a single string. You can try this same pattern (one scale tone, three open strings) on all six strings, if you like, as all the open strings are contained in the E natural minor scale.

FIG. 9.1. E Natural Minor Scale Open-String Exercise

Figure 9.2 follows the same idea as figure 9.1, except this time, I've moved over to the B string. Once again, it's a four-note pattern, but now, it's two fretted scale tones and two open strings. A good way to practice this is to find a speed that's challenging to you (but that you're in command of), and loop the four-bar pattern in a continuous circle.

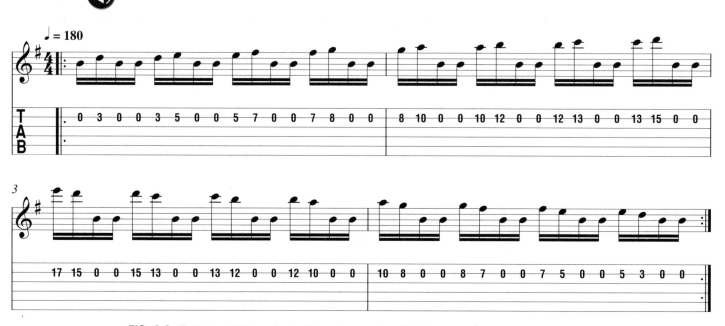

FIG. 9.2. E Natural Minor Scale Exercise on the B String

Figure 9.3 is a bit more difficult, as now, it's three scale tones and one open string. Synchronizing both hands and working this one up tempo-wise will take some time compared to the first two examples. As I've stated, it's helpful to play these on all your other strings. Also try combining all three examples to help you create your own melodic ideas.

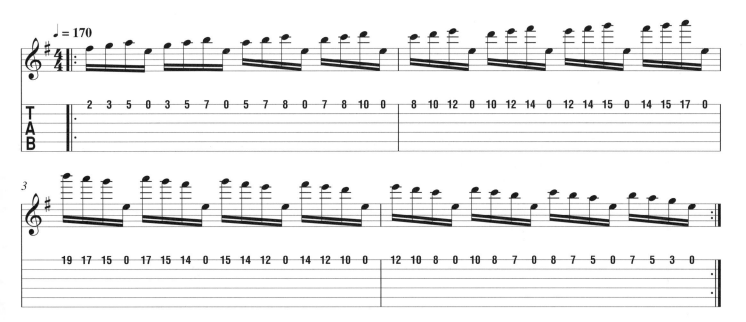

FIG. 9.3. E Natural Minor Scale Exercise, One Open String

In figure 9.4, I've shifted keys to G minor and also changed the rhythmic pattern from sixteenth notes to triplets. The basic idea of the exercise is the same, this time on the G string. I'm back to one fretted note, and since it's triplet based, two open strings. You can experiment playing these with varying degrees of palm muting, or use more of an open sound with no pick-hand muting at all.

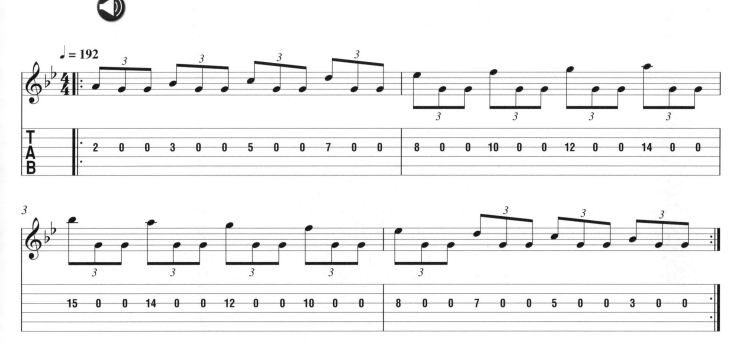

FIG. 9.4. G Minor Exercise in Triplets

Figure 9.5 follows suit with the previous examples. I'm again adding fretted notes to make the exercise more challenging as well as interesting. This time, it's climbing up the G minor scale three notes at a time, followed by three open strings. You can play all of these in any scale or any key containing open strings.

FIG. 9.5. G Minor Exercise in Triplets, Three Open Strings

Many of the European players that had a huge impact on my guitar playing (Ritchie Blackmore, Yngwie Malmsteen, Gary Moore, Michael Schenker, and Uli Jon Roth) utilized open-string ideas inside their solos as well as in the rhythm sections of their tunes. Examples 9.6 through 9.12 are much more solo-idea and tune-context based. They're also influenced to some extent by some of the players just mentioned.

Figure 9.6 is a simple idea in E minor moving down the scale on the top two strings alternating between one scale tone and one open string. It's in the E harmonic minor scale when moving to the B string. The whole lick is repeated in the second two bars before resolving with a slight variation. I'm alternate picking the entire lick, but you can also try playing it by picking the scale tone and then pulling off to the open string.

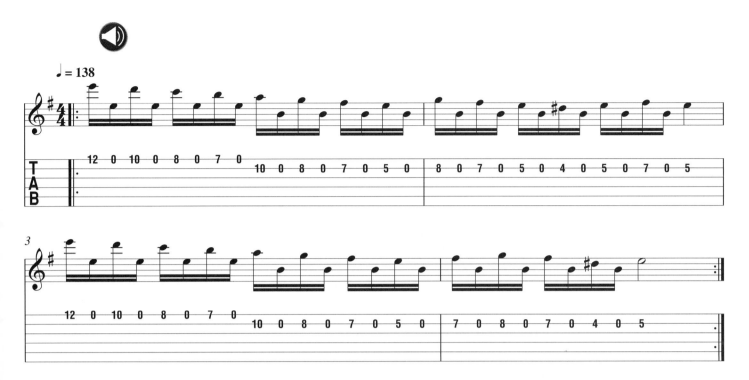

FIG. 9.6. E Harmonic Minor Exercise

Figure 9.7 is a very Ritchie Blackmore–inspired lick all inside the E natural minor scale. I use the same motif in each two-bar phrase. In bars 1 and 3, I'm alternate picking two scale tones, then playing two open strings. In bars 2 and 4, it's three scale tones and one open string. I especially like the way this one sounds with a slight palm mute on bars 1 and 3 of the lick, and then more of an open non-muted sound in bars 2 and 4. You could try it with any combination of either.

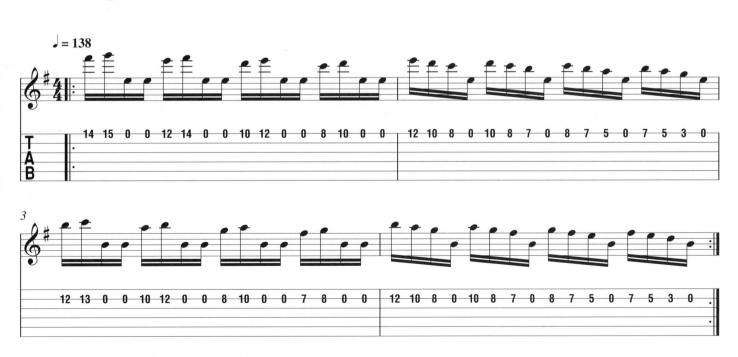

FIG. 9.7. E Natural Minor Scale Pattern

Figure 9.8. is a section of the *Psycho Shred Suite* ("Presto" movement) from my 2004 solo release, *Speed Metal Messiah*. It's a fast, triplet-based idea (inspired by Yngwie Malmsteen). In bars 1, 3, and 5, I'm using a melodic pattern combining the open E with moving about the scale in diatonic thirds. Both triplet motifs from previous examples 9.4 and 9.5 are included in this one (one scale tone on two open strings, and three scale tones on three open strings). In the last two bars, the lick resolves in E harmonic minor with a Baroque type of three-note single-string motif.

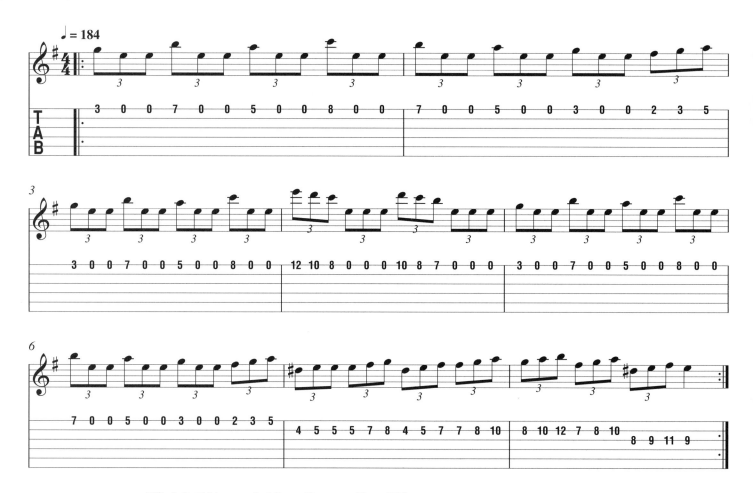

FIG. 9.8. E Harmonic Minor, Baroque Type Riff

Figure 9.9 is once again Blackmore inspired—a snake charmer/Eastern-sounding type of solo lick inside the E Hungarian minor scale. This works great played over a B major chord evoking the fifth mode of E Hungarian, known sometimes as B double harmonic minor (B, C, D♯, E, F♯, G, A♯, B). The hammer-ons, pull-offs, and half-step bends, in combination with the open B string, really give this lick a very unique sound and color.

FIG. 9.9. E Hungarian Minor Scale, Blackmore-Inspired Pattern

Figure 9.10 is a much more technically demanding neo-classical type of open-string section, utilizing the combination of open strings and classical arpeggios. The first two bars contain a very classical sounding A minor type of arpeggio, where in addition to the notes of the triad, I add G♯, the leading tone (raised 7th tone from A harmonic minor), and the second degree of the scale, B. In bar 5, I switch to a linear three-note harmonic minor based type of motif, and then in bar 6, combine the open string with a G♯ diminished 7 arpeggio. In bar 7, it's back to A minor, combining the open high E with the notes of the arpeggio, using a fairly demanding alternate-picked pattern in sixteenth-note triplets (sextuplets). Then, it's back to a neoclassical harmonic minor motif in combination with an octave jump.

Take note: the three open strings in the last three notes of beat 2, in both measures 8 and 10, will give you time to change position for the Paganini-inspired octave jump. Open strings can be a very effective way to change positions, register-wise.

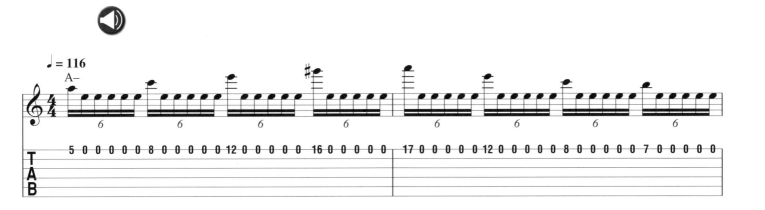

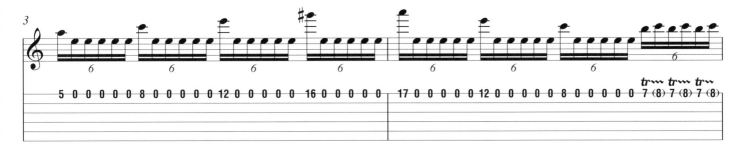

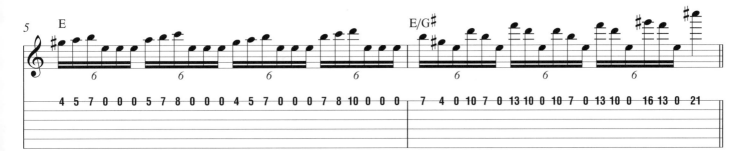

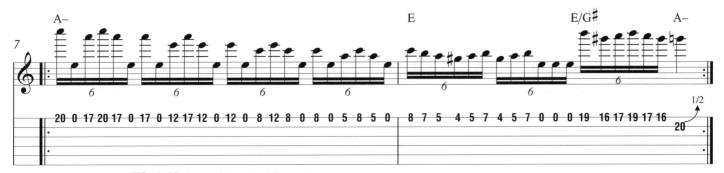

FIG. 9.10. Neo-Classical Exercise

Figure 9.11 is a small section of the track "Pistoleros" from my newest solo release, *Revenge of the Shredlord*. This is a sextuplet sixteenth-based melodic idea in A harmonic minor. In the first three bars, the simple motif is followed each time by two open E strings. Then in bar 4 (first ending), there's a two-string diminished-scale run, combining alternate picking with hammer-ons and pull-offs. The first two bars then repeat. In the second ending, the two-string diminished-scale run continues up the fretboard.

You might find playing this example completely evenly at tempo to be somewhat challenging. The combination of the open string motif and two-string scale run will certainly present a different type of synchronization for your pick hand.

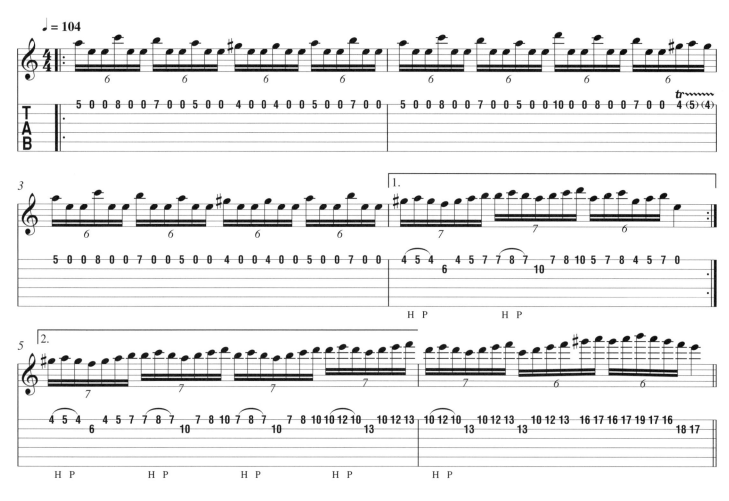

FIG. 9.11. Section from "Pistoleros"

Figure 9.12 is another section from *Revenge of the Shredlord.* This one's from the Bach/Blackmore–influenced ballad entitled "In the Master's House." In the first six bars, I'm combining open strings with an arpeggio-based melodic idea. The first two beats of bar 1 contain an A minor triad arpeggio, then G major on beats 3 and 4. In bar 2, the chord changes to C major, followed by a descending scale/open-string run. The first two beats of bar 3 are identical to the first bar. Then, on beats 3 and 4, there is a classically influenced harmonic minor motif that resolves to the A minor triad in bar 4. (Note: I'm using that classical sounding arpeggio in bar 4, the triad with the 2nd degree of the scale added to it.)

The first two bars are repeated in bars 5 and 6. In the last two bars, the section ends with a Baroque-influenced single-string scale run that resolves nicely in the final bar. This again is a prime example that something doesn't have to be technically complex to be effective and sound cool.

FIG. 9.12. Section from "In the Master's House"

In the final example, figure 9.13, I'm again combining open strings with arpeggio-based ideas, this time utilizing fretboard tapping. The sixteenth-note–based pattern is constant throughout the example, and each bar contains a different arpeggio, making this example fairly easy to memorize. The chord sequence is all inside a combination of the E natural and E harmonic minor scales. The entire example (except the final bar, where it resolves) is all played on the B string. Once you are able to execute the initial tapping pattern, just plug that into the single-string arpeggios, and off you go. This type of lick will help you to recognize arpeggios on a single string. Technically, it's a fairly pedestrian tapping pattern to get under your hands.

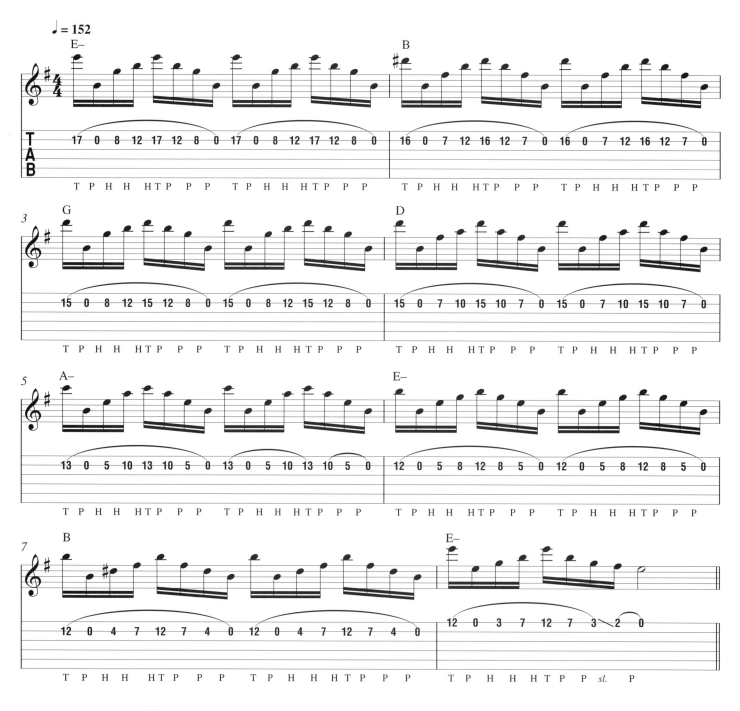

FIG. 9.13. Sixteenth-Note Based Pattern

CHAPTER 10

"Open-String Etude"

Chapter 9 contained quite a few open-string examples, some of the technique-building variety and many soloing-context types of ideas. In this chapter, I've transcribed a portion of "Sacrifice," a track from my release *Joe Stump's Reign of Terror* (2003), entitled "Conquer and Divide." This excerpt features several simple open-string motifs, as well as some two-string arpeggios.

The first eight bars (four bars repeated) are all inside the E natural minor scale. In bar 1, it's a melodic open-string motif moving about the scale in thirds. Then in bar 2, the last two beats use a technique covered in the previous chapter where I play a three-note scale run combined with the open E string. Bar 3 is just the first bar repeated, and it descends down the scale in bar 4.

In the next section, the chord changes to B major, and now we're inside the E harmonic minor scale. I move up the scale, alternate picking the entire time, pedaling off the open B string. In bar 2 of this section, I add in a straight descending four-note scale run. In the first ending, motif-wise, it's just like the beginning section in E minor where the third bar is just bar 1 of the section, repeated. Then in bar 2 of the first ending, it moves down the harmonic minor scale before ending on B. Following the ending and repeat signs, you go back to the first two bars again and then take the second ending that involves a tremolo-picked harmonic minor run that targets the chord tones of the B major triad.

The final section is all two-string arpeggios. This section is considerably more difficult than the previous two open-string sections. In bar 11, it's a two-string sweep pattern (picking down/down and then up on the second note on the top string). The picking pattern remains constant; the only thing that changes is the arpeggio shape. Please pay strict attention to the pick strokes notated.

Also, I'm using some palm muting on these first four shapes to help with tone and articulation. In measures 11–13, the chord sequence is E minor, C major, and then it goes to an A major chord with the third of the chord C# in the bass. Over this chord, I'm using a C# diminished triad arpeggio. After that, to D major, then to B/D# with a D# diminished arpeggio played over that chord.

In the next three bars, the arpeggio pattern changes to a more common, old-school, two-string lick using pull-offs in combination with consecutive down strokes. The E minor and C major shapes are different than the ones previously played; it's always helpful to be able to recognize triad arpeggios in all the different inversions and string combinations.

The final bar involves some note bending. First, I'm bending B up a half step to C, then the high C♯ bends up a whole step to the third of the B chord, D♯. Pay strict attention to your intonation and vibrato when note bending, making sure the pitches are in tune and that you're controlling them properly.

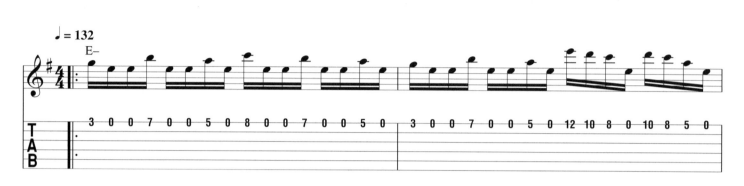

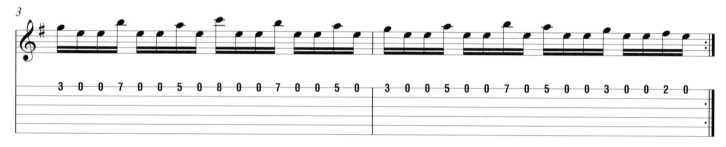

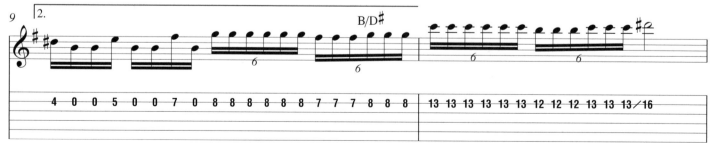

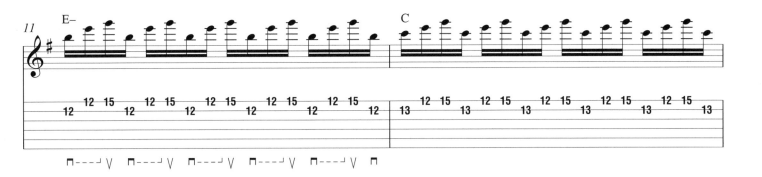

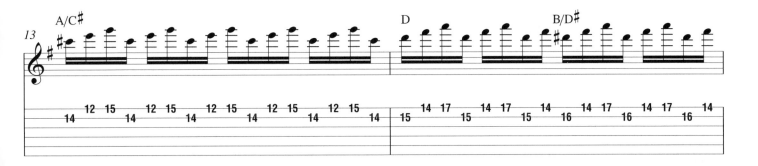

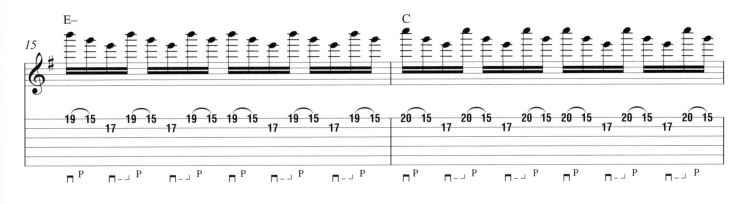

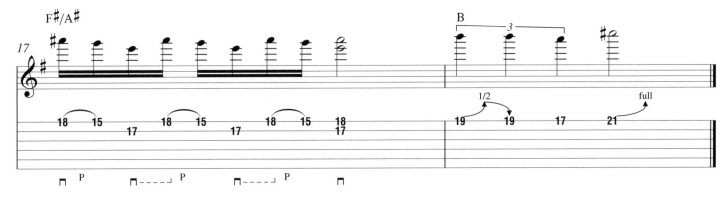

FIG. 10.1. "Open-String Etude"

CONCLUSION

This book covers quite a bit of material. Many of the topics are what I consider old-school staples of metal/shred guitar: double/tremolo picking, scale patterns, scale fragments, technique-building drills and etudes, arpeggio play, open-string techniques, etc.—important foundational stuff. While metal/shred guitar has evolved and changed in all kinds of ways over the years, many of these techniques have remained constant.

For those of you familiar with my playing and release catalogue, you know that there are many additional elements and aspects to my playing, such as classically influenced linear play, Baroque pedal point, extreme sweep/economy picking, harmonic minor, diminished licks/patterns, and Hungarian minor. While some of these topics were touched on in this book, I certainly could have had twice the amount of material, discussing many of these topics in far greater length and detail. I tried to make the book's content useful and helpful to players on all levels. No matter what style of metal/shred you play, I'm sure you'll find many more techniques that will improve your technical command, as well as expand your playing vocabulary.

ABOUT THE AUTHOR

Photo by Eddie Carlino

JOE STUMP

Shredlord Joe Stump has been raining down full-throttle shred/speed metal since his first solo offering *Guitar Dominance* was released in 1993. He is one of the most intense and over-the-top guitarists on the planet. His maniacal guitar-driven releases are amazing displays of power and jaw-dropping technical command. He was named by *Guitar One* magazine as one of the ten fastest shredders of all time, by *Guitar World* as one of the fifty fastest players of all time, and by *Guitarist* magazine as one of the top twenty shredders of all time. He has been featured in countless guitar-based and metal publications, fanzines, and webzines worldwide.

Stump has toured the world both as a solo artist and with power metal bands Joe Stump's Reign of Terror, Holy Hell, and Raven Lord. He is also an associate professor of guitar at the esteemed Berklee College of Music, where he's been the metal/shred guitar specialist for the last twenty years.